SIMPLE HOME REMEDIES

FOR

A HEALTHY LIFESTYLE

SIMPLE HOME REMEDIES
FOR
A HEALTHY LIFESTYLE

Anne McIntyre

Gaia Books Limited

A GAIA ORIGINAL

SIMPLE HOME REMEDIES

Conceived by Joss Pearson

® This is the Registered Trade Mark of
Gaia Books Limited.

First published in the United Kingdom in 1994 under the title Folk Remedies for Common Ailments by
Gaia Books Limited *and* 20 High Street,
66 Charlotte Street, Stroud, Glos GL5 1AS.
London W1P 1LR

This edition produced by TAJ Books Ltd 2002 for
Eagle Editions
11 Healthfield, Royston
Hertfordshire
SG8 5BW

ISBN 1-902328-38-8

Jacket design by bigmetalfish.com

Printed and bound in China

Caution
The techniques, ideas, and suggestions in this book are not intended as a substitute for proper medical advice. Any application of the techniques, ideas, and suggestions in this book is at the reader's sole discretion and risk.

To the reader: *The predicted benefits of herbalism are not so much based on conventional scientific study as on the observations of practitioners over many years of practice. Thus, where the text makes claims, for example, that a certain herb has diuretic properties, it normally means that this improvement has been observed in practice. While some sceptics might call it coincidence, herbalists believe that the results occur frequently and consistently enough to represent true healing effects. The techniques, ideas, and suggestions in the book are not intended as a substitute for medical advice. Any application of the techniques, ideas, and suggestions in the book is at the reader's sole discretion and risk.*

CONTENTS

INTRODUCTION

We have much to thank our ancestors for: their knowledge and insight into the successful use of indigenous minerals, foods, and plants as medicines have survived through generations to give us a rich global heritage of folklore.

It may come as a surprise to find that our kitchen cupboards, gardens, and hedgerows are packed with potent medicines for almost every ill. For thousands of years, humans have depended on local foods and herbs and have treated them with the respect they deserved. In the last century, modern drugs - the powerful "magic bullets" - have caused us to forget our simple, readily available remedies, relegating them to the ranks of cranky folk remedies or "old wives' tales" which lack the scientific proof that the 20th century demands. However, it is unfair to dismiss folk remedies in this way. Scientists worldwide are researching foods and herbs in their search for "new cures" for ills such as heart disease and cancer. They are making exciting discoveries, and identifying chemically active ingredients within many folk cures which explain their ancient use. Remedies such as cabbage juice for arthritis, onion for the heart, garlic for infections, and apples for gout, have been found to have scientific merit after all; to have a basis in fact and not merely romance. This is not surprising when you consider that many major medical discoveries come from nature - penicillin from bread mould, digoxin from foxglove, and aspirin from willow.

So it looks like folklore is here to stay. It is inexpensive, practical, readily available, and - most importantly - it works!

TREATING COMMON AILMENTS

The treatment of common ailments begins at home, and in many cases this still involves an interesting variety of old folk remedies. A salt gargle makes an effective cure for sore throats; hot lemon and honey drinks ease colds and catarrh; vinegar soothes wasp stings; and dock leaves rubbed on to nettle stings provide ready relief. Knowledge of this vast array of medicines, be they sitting in your larder, growing among your fruit and vegetables, or just simply there in your garden, will enable you to provide the right remedy for most ailments, ranging from acute infections and minor upsets, to chronic disorders and first-aid problems.

Folk remedies are gifts from nature, the majority being either herbs or plant foods. Plants have always been central to our lives, and have played an important part in mythology and religious ceremonies. They are the source of the foods we enjoy and the air we breathe, and so it is hardly surprising that for thousands of years they have also supplied us with remedies for treating almost every ill. Despite the move in the 19th and 20th centuries toward technological medicine and the use of sophisticated drugs, traditional plant remedies still provide about 85 per cent of the world's medicines, and are just as valuable today as they ever were. With their myriad therapeutic properties, they can provide safe, effective, and time-proven alternatives to orthodox drugs when used appropriately. They make excellent preventive medicines and can enhance general well-being when taken in conjunction with a healthy diet and lifestyle. They can also bring symptomatic relief (for example, for first aid and minor infections such as coughs, colds, and sore throats), to avoid the use of drugs such as antibiotics. Better still, you can use them in the context of a holistic approach to healing, where physical symptoms are viewed in relation to other factors, including emotions, stress, attitudes, the social, domestic, and working environment, relationships, diet, relaxation, and exercise. All play a part in the emergence of an individual disease pattern.

A few words of advice

Ideally, before using folk remedies, you should strive to understand your symptoms and, if necessary, visit your local medical practitioner or herbalist for a clear diagnosis. If acute symptoms do not clear within a few days, and chronic symptoms do not improve within 3-4 weeks, call in professional help. Human bodies are supremely well adapted to metabolize plant constituents as they occur in nature, so there is little risk of side effects or aggravations when using folk remedies.

However, it is important that all plant remedies are used in as natural a state as possible, free from chemical sprays and other human pollutants. When picking herbs, always gather away from roadsides and cultivated land that may have been sprayed. Be careful also not to overpick the same area or gather from places where the plant is scarce, and avoid any plant that looks stunted or diseased. Always choose free-range eggs, and for remedies that are based on fruits and vegetables, try to obtain them as fresh as you can and, wherever possible, organically grown. Eat them raw or lightly cooked, with their skins intact to derive optimum benefit. Finally, never cook in aluminium pots. The correct handling of folk remedies will help ensure their beneficial effects and enhance their ability to provide medicines.

PREPARATIONS FOR INTERNAL USE

All you have to do with many of the remedies is eat them. Carrots, oats, apples, barley, and cabbage, for example, are common ingredients in a wide variety of recipes, but you can be creative and add interest to your diet by including some of the more unusual remedies in your daily fare. Try adding borage flowers to summer drinks, dandelion leaves to your salads and sandwiches, or even marigold flowers to enliven and beautify an otherwise ordinary salad. Don't be afraid to experiment!

Tea

You can prepare a tea either as an infusion or a decoction. Choose the infusion method to prepare teas when using the soft aerial parts of the plants, such as the flowers, stems, and leaves. Use the decoction method to prepare more woody materials, such as roots, bark, and seeds.

Infusions

These are prepared just like Chinese or Indian teas. Make a standard adult dose with 28g (1oz) of dried herb to 600ml (1 pint) of water or a teaspoonful per cup. Double the amount if the plant is fresh. You can vary this according to taste, and halve or quarter it for children. Place the plant in a warm pot, pour on boiling water, and cover to prevent beneficial essential oils from escaping to the atmosphere. Leave to infuse for about 10 minutes and strain. You can either drink it immediately or store it in the refrigerator in an airtight container for up to two days. Alternatively, you can use tea bags of these remedies if they are available from local health food stores.

Plants with a high mucilage content such as comfrey leaf need to be made up as cold infusions, otherwise you risk destroying their therapeutic constituents. Pour cold water over the plant and leave to infuse for 10–12 hours. Generally it is best to take infusions hot by the cupful three times daily in chronic problems, increasing to once an hour (or 2-hourly) in acute illness. Children will only be able to take little amounts at a time, so administer small doses regularly and often. For urinary tract disorders, it is best to drink infusions luke-warm to cold. If you find certain remedies unpalatable, try combining several herbs together, so that aromatic herbs such as peppermint, lavender, and lemon balm disguise the taste, or use licorice, aniseed, unsweetened fruit juices, or honey to flavour infusions.

Decoctions

The hard, woody parts of the plant have tough cell walls that require great heat to break them down before they can impart their constituents to water. Break the plant into small pieces by chopping, crushing, or hammering. Use the same proportions of plant to water as when making infusions, and then add a little more water to make up for slight loss, through evaporation, during preparation. Place the plant in a saucepan (not aluminium), and cover with cold water. Bring to the boil, cover, and simmer for 10-15 minutes. Strain, flavour, or sweeten as for infusions, and drink hot by the cupful three times daily for a chronic problem, and up to once hourly for an acute illness.

Syrups

You can use syrups to make remedies more palatable, especially for children, or even squeamish adults. Pour 600ml (1 pint) of boiling water over 1.25kg (2.75lb) of soft brown sugar and stir over a gentle heat until all the sugar has dissolved and the solution comes to the boil. If you have herbal tinctures, you can mix 1 part tincture to 3 parts syrup and this will keep indefinitely. If you prepare an infusion or decoction, add 325g (12oz) of sugar to 600ml (1 pint) of the liquid and heat until all the sugar dissolves. Cool and store in the refrigerator. Generally give a dessertspoonful to a child 3-4 times daily in chronic problems, and double the dose in acute illness.

Medicinal honeys

These are a delicious and very easy way to give remedies to children. Finely chop or powder the fresh or dried plants, and cover with honey. Leave to infuse for a few minutes before administering them on a teaspoon. You can also give essential oils in honey - one drop per teaspoonful of honey.

Tinctures

A mixture of water and alcohol is used to extract the chemical components from the plant and to act as a preservative, making a more concentrated extract. It has a shelf life of at least two years. The ratio of water to alcohol ranges from 25 per cent alcohol for tannins to 90 per cent alcohol for resins and gums. You can use the plant fresh or dried, either finely chopped or powdered. Place it in a large jar and pour the alcohol and water solution over it. A standard preparation requires one part dried herb to five parts fluid, while fresh plants can be used at a ratio of 1:2. To make 1 litre (2.2 pints) of chamomile tincture, take 200g (7oz) of dried herb and pour over it 1 litre (2.2 pints) of brandy or vodka. Seal in an airtight container and leave to macerate out of direct sunlight for at least two weeks, shaking the jar daily. Then press through a muslin bag (or use a simple wine press), squeezing out as much fluid as you can, before discarding the herb (it makes excellent compost). Pour the tincture into a dark storage jar and keep it cool.

Alternatively, you can use equal parts of glycerol and water to make a syrup-like tincture that is particularly suitable for children. Give 1 teaspoonful three times daily after meals in chronic cases, doubling the dose for acute illness. Use between 10 drops and half a teaspoonful for children. Dilute with water or fruit juice of your choice.

Juices

Juice extracted from several remedies provides a concentrate, easily assimilated by the body. Cabbage juice, for example, is excellent for relieving peptic ulcers, gastritis, heart burn, and ulcerative colitis.

Throat sprays

Dilute either 1 teaspoonful of tincture or 5 drops of essential oil in half a cup of water or use half a cup of infusion or decoction. Fill a throat spray with this liquid and spray once every 2 hours in acute infections, and three times daily in chronic problems.

Gargle

Dilute 1 teaspoonful of tincture in half a cup of water, or use half a cup of infusion or decoction, and gargle every 2 hours in acute infections, and 2-3 times daily in chronic problems. Gargle with your head back, holding the liquid in your throat and saying "Aaaah" for a few seconds before spitting the liquid out. Repeat until the liquid is completely finished.

Mouthwash

Use 1 teaspoonful of tincture diluted in half a cup of water, or half a cup of infusion or decoction. Rinse it thoroughly around the mouth and then spit it out. Repeat until the liquid is finished. Do this three times daily.

PREPARATIONS FOR EXTERNAL USE

Many ingredients of remedies are easily absorbed through the skin.

Baths

Either add a couple of drops of essential oil to the water (use dilute oils for babies and children), hang a muslin bag with fresh or dried aromatic herbs under the hot tap, or add strong herbal infusions or decoctions to the bath water, before immersing yourself in it for 10-30 minutes. The essential oils are absorbed through the skin's pores and inhaled.

Hand and foot baths

Use a few drops of essential oil, a litre of strong infusion or decoction, or a few teaspoonfuls of tincture in a bowl of hot water and take a foot bath for 8 minutes in the evening and a hand bath for the same length of time in the morning. This is an excellent way to give remedies to babies and children.

Ointments, creams, and lotions

The following simple recipe tells you how to make an ointment using fresh or dried ingredients. Macerate as much of the required remedy as you can in 450ml (16floz) of olive oil and 50g (2oz) of beeswax, and heat gently for a few hours in a bain-marie, during which time the chemicals in the remedy will be taken up by the oil. Then press the oil through a muslin bag, and pour it while still warm into ointment jars. You can make creams very easily by mixing either a little tincture, decoction, infusion, or a few drops of essential oil into a base of aqueous cream. Apply ointments and creams 2-3 times a day to treat skin problems, varicose veins, and sore or inflamed joints.

You can make lotions by mixing dilute tinctures, infusions, or decoctions, or a few drops of essential oils, with water. Apply them externally, 2-3 times daily, for skin problems, varicose veins, and for various first aid treatments.

Compresses

Using either a hot or cold infusion, decoction, dilute tincture, or a few drops of essential oil in water, soak a clean cloth or flannel, then wring it out and apply to the affected part. Repeat applications several times for good effect.

Poultices

You can make poultices with either fresh or dried ingredients. First, bruise all the fresh material (leaves, stems, roots) or finely chop or powder the dried ingredients, before adding water to mix into a paste. Then place the remedy between two pieces of gauze and bind it to the affected part with a cotton bandage, and keep it warm with a hot water bottle if you can. Leave in place for several hours, and repeat morning and night. A bread poultice will bring a boil to a head, while a cabbage leaf poultice will help to relieve swollen arthritic joints.

Liniments

A liniment, or rubbing oil, is made up of medicinal extracts in an oil or alcohol base, or a mixture of oils and alcohol tinctures of the chosen remedies. Liniments usually contain stimulating essential oils, ginger, or cayenne, to increase local circulation and enhance absorption through the skin.

Medicinal oils

Although you have to buy essential oils, you can make medicinal oils by macerating freshly chopped plants in pure vegetable oil for about two weeks. Cabbage leaves steeped in olive oil make an excellent remedy for chilblains, chapped skin, and boils.

Place the ingredients in a glass jar with a tight-fitting lid, cover with oil, and put it on a sunny window sill. Shake the jar daily. The oil will take the components of the remedy. After 2 weeks, filter off the oil and squeeze the remainder through a muslin bag. Store in a dark bottle in a cool place.

Room spray

Dissolve 5-10 drops of essential oil in a little water and put into a plant spray or an atomizer. Spray the room every few hours if you are ill in bed, or last thing at night before you retire.

Steam treatment/facial steamer

Dissolve 5-10 drops of essential oil in a bowl of hot water or a facial steamer or use a hot infusion/decoction. Lean over the bowl or steamer, and allow the steam to seep into your skin for 5-10 minutes. Repeat twice a week for skin problems, such as acne.

Vaporizers

These are available from some health food stores and pharmacies or essential oil suppliers (see p.93). Put a little water into the clay bowl and add 10 drops of your chosen essential oil or blend of a few. Insert a nightlight under the clay bowl - the heat helps the oil to evaporate.

Eyewash/eyebath

Half-fill an eyebath with a lukewarm-to-cool decoction. Hold the eyebath firmly over your open eye and put your head back. Move your head from side to side for a few seconds so that the remedy rinses the eye thoroughly. Then discard the liquid, wash the eyebath, and use the decoction for the other eye. Repeat every 2 hours in acute eye infections, and three times daily for chronic problems.

Juice

The fresh juice of many remedies can be applied directly to the skin. Borage juice, for example, exudes from the leaves when it is rubbed on to the skin to soothe burns, bites, and stings. The juice of dock leaves is famous for relieving nettle stings.

Sleep pillow

Choose a mixture of relaxing dried herbs, and sprinkle them with a few drops of your favourite oil. Use them to fill a small bag or pillow case and place it by your head or under your pillow so that you inhale the therapeutic aromas while you sleep.

FROM THE KITCHEN CUPBOARD

The kingdom of heaven is like to a grain of mustard seed, which a man took, and sowed in his field: which indeed is the least of all seeds: but when it is grown, it is the greatest among herbs, and becometh a tree, so that the birds of the air come and lodge in the branches thereof.

The Bible (St. Matthew 13:31)

Happy the age, to which we moderns give the name of 'golden', when men choose to live on woodland fruits; and for their medicines took Herbs from the field, and Simples from the brook.

Ovid (Metamorphoses Lib. XV)

When asked by the scholar "What is an herb?", the Emperor Charlemagne replied "The friend of physicians and the praise of cooks".

CINNAMON

A Tonic to the Whole System

Properties

Strengthening tonic • Warming • Antiseptic • Sedative • Astringent

Delicious and aromatic, cinnamon is a wonderful warming and strengthening remedy to dispel cold, winter chills, and symptoms associated with cold, congestion, and deficiency of vital energy. Both types of cinnamon have been used since time immemorial to treat diarrhoea, rheumatism, hypertension, abdominal pains, and female problems.

Internal

A hot drink of cinnamon stimulates the circulation and causes sweating, preventing or resolving flu, colds, catarrh, fevers, and infections. You can inhale oil of cinnamon for head colds and chest infections. Cinnamon's warming and stimulating properties can be given direction in the body by combining it with other remedies: with thyme, hyssop, or elecampane for bronchial congestion and infection; with angelica and blue cohosh as a uterine remedy to treat irregular and painful periods, heavy bleeding, infections, and leucorrhoea. Cinnamon warms and stimulates the digestive system, improving digestion and calming colic, diarrhoea, nausea, wind, and distension. Its tannins stem bleeding in nose bleeds, heavy periods, and resolve catarrh. The essential oil in *Cinnamomum zeylanicum* is one of the strongest natural antiseptics known. Its antibacterial, antifungal, and antiviral properties prevent and treat acute infections, including cystitis, colds, bronchitis, thrush and enteritis, ME, and chronic infections, such as candidiasis and tonsillitis. Eugenol in the oil acts as an anaesthetic, helping to relieve pain in arthritis, headaches, muscle pain, and toothache when applied locally.

External

Cinnamon makes a good antiseptic wash for cuts, wounds, bites and stings, head lice, and infective skin complaints.

Folk remedies from the past

Cinnamon bark has been a highly prized spice for millennia, at times more valuable than gold. Cinnamon is mentioned in the Bible and was used in ancient Egypt for embalming and witchcraft. The Crusaders brought cinnamon to western Europe to flavour food and medicines, and for perfumes. In medieval Europe it was recommended as an aphrodisiac.

- Cinnamon powder stirred into a glass of milk is an old country cure for dysentery.
- As a strengthening tonic, cinnamon has been used to relieve fatigue, debility, melancholy, winter lethargy, poor circulation, impotence, and nervous problems.
- Cinnamon was prescribed as a remedy for cholera, at the beginning of mumps, and for consumptives as an inhalant.

CAUTION

Do not use during pregnancy.

WATERCRESS

An Excellent Tonic for Mind and Body

Properties

Stimulant • Tonic • Antiseptic • Expectorant • Depurative • Detoxifying

Rich in vitamins, minerals, and trace elements, watercress makes a nourishing tonic for those who feel stressed and run down. Not only does it restore nutrients and provide iron for anaemia, it also enhances immunity and increases vitality. Apparently, the Egyptian kings gave watercress juice to their slaves twice a day to increase their productivity!

Internal

Watercress is both pungent and bitter, making it an excellent blood cleanser, aiding the body's elimination of toxins. The pungent quality is warming and stimulating; it invigorates digestion, improves appetite and absorption, and increases circulation. The detoxifying bitters stimulate liver, pancreas, and gall bladder activity, enhancing enzyme secretion and helping to ensure normal bowel function and blood sugar levels. Watercress also acts on the kidneys and bladder as a diuretic and it dissolves stones and gravel. As a blood cleanser, watercress is excellent for arthritis, rheumatism, and gout (by eliminating uric acid), and for combatting skin problems such as eczema and psoriasis, as well as such eruptive infections as measles and chicken pox. It has antiseptic and expectorant properties, excellent for clearing chest infections, catarrh, and sinusitis. It also reduces fevers and lymphatic congestion, and may even have anti-tumour activity. The high vitamin E content may explain why it is thought to enhance fertility, increase sexual energy, and stimulate menstruation and lactation.

External

As an antiseptic watercress can be applied as a poultice to wounds, boils, ulcers, and skin infections such as cold sores and scabies. An infusion makes a good lotion for haemorrhoids and rashes, and a mouthwash for toothache.

Folk remedies from the past

So well did people feel after eating watercress that it was revered for its mystical intelligence – for drawing those elements vital to health from the earth. The Romans believed it even conferred intelligence on those who ate it.

• Parkinson in 1640 said that the crushed leaves or juice applied to the face removed freckles, pimples, and spots, and when mixed with vinegar relieved lethargy.

• North American Indians ate watercress to dissolve gravel and stones in the bladder.

• In the Middle Ages, people rubbed the juice into the scalp to strengthen the hair.

Chewing raw watercress strengthens gums and helps prevent bleeding.

CAUTION

Do not eat watercress found near sheep: if contaminated by droppings it can transmit liver flukes.

HONEY

A Symbol of Goodness, Abundance, and the Sweet Things in Life

Properties

Expectorant • Antiseptic • Disinfectant

Folk remedies from the past

The word "honey" is derived from the Hebrew ghoneg, meaning delight. In the Bible, the land of Canaan supposedly flowed with milk and honey.

• The Teutons of Europe prepared wine from honey and then drank it for 30 days after marriage – hence the word "honeymoon". Perhaps honey's reputation as an aphrodisiac stems from this custom.

• Until World War I wounds were often treated with honey to disinfect them and speed healing.

• Rose honey was made with the juice of rose petals and given to the sick as a revitalizing tonic.

Take traces of pollen in local honey for several weeks prior to and during the hay fever season to desensitize you to pollen in your area.

Honey is highly nutritious and provides an easily assimilated food – particularly beneficial if you are weak or run down during or after illness. It contains predigested sugars, vitamins B and C, iron, magnesium, calcium, sodium, silica, manganese, and potassium. The sugars in honey provide energy and have a calming effect, stimulating serotonin production, which quietens brain activity, induces relaxation and sleep, and may help relieve the pain of headaches, neuralgia, and arthritis.

Internal

Honey's expectorant action has long been used for coughs and catarrh. Mixed with lemon or cider vinegar, honey makes a soothing cough syrup, and hot lemon and honey is a famous remedy for colds and fevers. Honey makes an excellent medium for giving herbs medicinally. One teaspoonful of chopped thyme in honey can be taken for coughs, bronchitis, whooping cough, and asthma. Honey provides a speedy cure for congestion, catarrh, and sinusitis, and makes a fine remedy for hay fever and allergic rhinitis. Research shows honey's potent antiseptic properties will help safeguard against infections including salmonella, cholera, typhoid and pneumococcus; honey is an excellent remedy for infective diarrhoea and vomiting. Insomnia sufferers may find relief if they take a teaspoon of honey at bedtime.

External

Honey is an antiseptic and speeds the healing of wounds including mouth and varicose ulcers. Honey is hygroscopic – it draws water to it and so can draw poisons and pus out of an infected wound or ulcer, or bring boils to a head. Honey also makes a healing remedy for burns and mastitis.

Since the time of the ancient Egyptians, honey has been praised for its medicinal virtues. Honey is mentioned 500 times in the Smith Papyrus, an Egyptian medical text from 2600–2200 BC. It was used as an antiseptic to heal wounds and ulcers, for coughs and fevers, and for embalming the dead. Modern scientific research has verified honey's potent antiseptic properties and its ability to inhibit infecting organisms – including those causing acute diarrhoea and dysentery. The remedy has the blessing of the World Health Organization which includes honey in its recipe for traveller's diarrhoea.

OATS

A Nerve Tonic and Body Builder!

Properties

Soothing • Laxative • Nerve tonic • Uterine tonic • Hypoglycaemic

A wonderfully nutritious food, oats are full of protein, calcium, magnesium, silicon, potassium, iron, and vitamins, and make an excellent energy-giving food. The body-building nutrients help make strong bones and teeth, and are vital for a healthy nervous system. Oats are one of the finest restorative remedies for the nervous system and can be helpful when withdrawing from tranquillizers and anti-depressant drugs.

Internal

Since they are easily digested, oats are ideal during chronic illness, convalescence, or following childbirth. Oat porridge and gruel, often made with spices, sugar, lemon, or wine, are time-honoured recipes for the invalid and elderly. Oats also have a reputation as a uterine tonic and for helping to overcome sterility and impotence. They are thought to stimulate the thyroid gland and have been shown to regulate oestrogen levels. Recent research has discovered that oat fibre can significantly lower blood cholesterol, helping to combat cardiovascular disease; it can also help high blood pressure, obesity, varicose veins, and haemorrhoids. Oats are helpful to diabetics since they lower blood sugar, and are also useful for reducing fluid retention. Oat fibre soothes the digestive tract and produces bulkier stools, speeding their passage through the bowel and reducing the exposure of the gut lining to irritants and carcinogens. Thus, they are thought to protect against the development of bowel cancer.

External

Oatmeal makes a good facial scrub, and is healing and soothing to sore and inflamed skin conditions.

Folk remedies from the past

Oats are well known as a nerve tonic to treat depression, debility, and nervous exhaustion.

• The relaxing properties of oats are evident from the traditional remedy for children and insomniacs of sleeping on a mattress stuffed with oat husks.

• Oats have been used as a soothing remedy for irritated conditions of the digestive tract and problems such as diverticulitis, irritable bowel syndrome, gastritis, and constipation.

To make cinnamon porridge, add 1 cup of oats to 2 cups of water. Bring to the boil and simmer until the oats are soft. Add $^1/_2$ teaspoonful of powdered cinnamon and serve immediately.

GINGER

A Wonderful Winter Warmer

Properties

Antioxidant • Antiseptic • Expectorant • Stimulant • Relaxant
Detoxifying • Digestive

The thick, tuberous roots of this reed-like plant have been used as a culinary spice and medicine since antiquity. Cultivated widely in the tropics, ginger is a warming remedy for warding off winter chills and fighting off infections before they become entrenched. Its antiseptic, volatile oils activate immunity, so making ginger a preventive remedy against colds, tonsillitis, bronchitis, and digestive infections.

Internal

Ginger stimulates the heart and circulation, creating a feeling of warmth and well-being, and restoring vitality. Hot ginger tea taken at the onset of a cold or flu, when you feel tired, chilly, and achy, promotes perspiration, brings down a fever, and helps clear toxins and catarrh. It also acts as an expectorant in the lungs, expelling phlegm and clearing chest infections. In India, fresh ginger tea is given to children for whooping cough. Ginger enhances digestion, invigorating the stomach and intestines, and promoting enzyme secretion. It is an excellent remedy for nausea, whether during pregnancy or from travel sickness. It soothes indigestion, clears toxins from the gut, calms wind, spasms, and griping with diarrhoea. In the uterus it promotes menstruation, useful for delayed and scanty periods, relieves pain, and is used to invigorate the reproductive system and treat impotence caused by deficiency of vital body warmth. Research has found that ginger inhibits blood clotting, lowers cholesterol, reduces blood pressure, and has antioxidant effects that slow the ageing process.

External

You can chew fresh ginger to dull the pain of toothache. Dilute ginger oil can be used in massage oils and liniments for lumbago, neuralgia, and painful joints.

Folk remedies from the past

Ginger is mentioned in Chinese medical texts dating back 2000 years, and was included in many Oriental prescriptions.

• Ginger has an ancient reputation as an aphrodisiac – men have claimed that it transforms frigid women into enchantresses.

• Around 1600, Lord Zouche brought ginger to England. His friend, the herbalist Gerard, reported that ginger "heateth and drieth in the iii degree", and recommended it as a warming aid to digestion.

• In the past, high blood pressure was reduced by applying a paste of powdered ginger and cold water to the forehead. Now, thankfully, adding ginger to your cooking is considered sufficient.

CAUTION

Because of its warmth ginger is not advised for those who do not tolerate heat, or have gastritis or peptic ulcers.

LEMON

A Refreshing Remedy for Warding off Infections

Properties

Tonic • Antiseptic • Diuretic • Astringent • Antioxidant • Detoxifying

Folk remedies from the past

The Romans used the lemon as an antidote to all poisons, but the fruit is more famous for its ability to prevent scurvy due to the high vitamin C and bioflavonoid content.

• Lemons were used to treat migraines and malaria, when taken in coffee.

• The juice of 3-4 lemons taken daily was a remedy for excessive menstruation.

• As a means of preventing arteriosclerosis, Russian folklore recommended everyone over 40 years of age to drink the juice of one lemon and one orange in hot water every morning.

To treat coughs, colds, and flu, add lemon juice to 3 cloves and honey in hot water.

For thousands of years lemons have been praised as a food and medicine. The antioxidant properties of the high vitamin C content make lemons helpful in speeding healing, retarding the signs of ageing, and warding off cancer.

Internal

Although lemons are generally regarded as acidic, during digestion the acids are metabolized to produce potassium carbonate, which helps to neutralize excess acidity and protect the lining of the digestive tract. This makes lemons helpful for many digestive problems including hiccoughs, heartburn, nausea, constipation, and worms. Lemons act as a tonic to the liver, stimulating bile production when the juice is taken in hot water one hour before breakfast each morning. Mixed with olive oil, lemon juice helps dissolve gall stones and even a fish bone stuck in the throat! It is also used to dissolve uric acid. Lemon juice is powerfully antiseptic, providing a boost to the immune system, an effective remedy for all kinds of infections, and it helps to bring down fevers. As a gargle, it relieves sore throats and tonsillitis. One tablespoon of juice in water half an hour before each meal can help relieve asthma. Lemon's antifungal properties make it a valuable cure for thrush. As a cleansing and diuretic remedy, lemon juice can be used for water retention, arthritis, and rheumatism.

External

Lemon juice's astringent action stems bleeding. Apply it on cotton wool to the nostrils for nose bleeds and massage bleeding gums with it in the morning and at night. Lemon juice also makes a good lotion to prevent sunburn. Mixed equally with glycerine, it soothes chapped lips, helps keep the complexion clear, and tones greasy skin.

Originally grown in India and Burma, lemons have been prized for their detoxifying properties. The juice is powerfully antiseptic, stimulating the immune system and promoting sweating – so making it an effective remedy for infections and fevers. Lemon's astringent action checks bleeding and relieves diarrhoea.

The tonic properties of lemons are also present in the pulp, which act to stimulate the system causing sweating and cleansing the body of poisons. The peel of the lemon contains pectin, the essential setting agent needed to make preserves and jams. Pectin also lowers cholesterol.

POTATO

A Nutritious yet Underestimated Staple

Properties

Antioxidant • Antiviral • Anti-inflammatory • Digestive

Even though Sir Walter Raleigh first planted the tubers of this South American plant on his Irish estate in the 16th century, it took 200 years for the potato to be commonly accepted as an edible vegetable. In England, people's suspicions were based on its connections with the nightshade family: certainly, its green parts share the same narcotic and poisonous properties, as do tubers which have turned green. However, this should not detract from the fact that, with its skin intact, it is a highly nutritious and energy-rich food, containing proteins, carbohydrate, vitamins (particularly B complex and C), minerals, and trace elements.

Internal

When baked or steamed in its skin, the potato retains much of its nutritional value and is easily digested. Since it contains almost no fat, it is an excellent energy source for slimmers. However, it is the juice of raw potato that is mostly used in folk medicine, traditionally for digestive problems – indigestion, colic, gastritis, peptic ulcers, liver disorders, gall stones, constipation, and as an antacid. Recent research suggests that the potato contains certain chemicals which may be effective against viruses and cancer. The skin has antioxidant properties, neutralizing the destructive free radicals involved in a variety of degenerative diseases, and thereby slowing the ageing process.

External

Raw potato juice soothes inflammation and encourages healing of skin infections, chronic dermatitis, wounds, and ulcers. A grated potato, mixed with olive oil, has been used successfully to treat burns, sunburn, cracked skin, and swollen eyelids. Slices of raw potato make a good poultice for sores and chilblains, and, when applied to the temples, headaches and migraine.

Folk remedies from the past

Potato is a traditional remedy for the heart and circulation. Russian folk medicine recommends that all those over 40 should grate a medium-sized raw potato and eat it daily before breakfast to delay the onset of arteriosclerosis.

• An old remedy for worms involved eating an evening meal of potato salad with walnut oil for three consecutive days.

• In Russia, suppositories cut from fresh potatoes and inserted into the anus were used for quick relief of haemorrhoids.

• Raw potato juice and hot potato water used to be applied to the painful area in gout, rheumatism, and lumbago.

For high blood pressure, boil the skins of 4–5 potatoes in 600ml (1 pint) of water for 15 minutes. Drink 1–2 cupfuls of the strained and cooled liquid daily.

SALT

A Vital Nutrient, Tonic, and Stimulant

Properties

Stimulant • Emetic • Cleanser • Antiseptic • Digestive • Laxative

The human body contains about 250g (8.75oz) of sodium chloride, which is present in the blood plasma, lymph, saliva, and sweat. It is excreted mostly in urine and sweat. Its main function is to hold water in the body by osmotic pressure and to aid the transport of carbon dioxide in the blood.

Internal

In small amounts, salt stimulates digestion and secretion of digestive enzymes and as such makes a good tonic and stimulant. Salt has been used as an emetic to cleanse the stomach of toxins and reduce catarrh. It also makes a good purgative when taken as a saline solution. Salt depletion can occur after vomiting, diarrhoea, or in those whose appetite is depressed. It can also occur from excessive sweating in a hot climate, causing breathlessness and cramp. A saline solution administered intravenously or by mouth will remedy the situation, and this treatment is also used for shock, collapse due to haemorrhage, and in uraemia.

Salt has long been used not only to flavour but also to preserve food. But, as a word of warning, manufacturers add salt to most processed foods, so that we consume far more than we need. If the kidneys have difficulty in clearing excess salt via the urine, fluid retention and high blood pressure may result. This pattern is often set in childhood with a high-salt diet.

External

For sore throats, enlarged adenoids, inflamed gums, and mouth ulcers, use a weak salt solution (1 teaspoonful of salt in a glass of warm water) as a mouthwash and gargle – its cleansing and antiseptic action will check the growth of infection. At the onset of a cold, use a gargle and nasal cleansing (drawing salt water through the nose).

Folk remedies from the past

The word "salt" has a sense of great value. The expression "worth his salt" refers back to Roman times when soldiers were paid in salt money. Salt was also highly prized by the ancient Greeks – Homer went so far as to call it "divine".

• In medieval feasts, "inferior" guests sat below the midway point on the table marked by a pot of salt. Only those above the salt were invited to savour its delights.

• In India Ayurvedic physicians believe that salt stimulates fire (pitta) and accentuates feelings of energy and aggression.

• A salt enema (2 tablespoons of salt to 600ml (1 pint) of warm water) used to be given to children to rid them of threadworms.

As a rule of thumb, take less sodium chloride in your food and replace it with potassium salts.

PEPPER

A Fiery Remedy to Invigorate the System and Enhance Immunity

Properties

Pungent • Stimulant • Digestive • Immune-enhancer • Rubefacient • Decongestant
Expectorant • Anaesthetic

Folk remedies from the past

Pepper was used as a remedy for infections, such as scarlet fever, dysentery, typhus, cholera, smallpox, and bubonic plague, and to relieve the pain and swelling of arthritic joints.

• So valuable was pepper considered that Attila the Hun demanded, among other things, more than a ton of black pepper as a ransom for the city of Rome.

• In the Middle Ages, pepper was worth its weight in gold – literally.

• The Japanese added cayenne to remedies for infertility, while the Indonesians used it as a folk remedy to procure abortion.

• The ancient Greek and Roman physicians used – and we continue to use – cayenne as a "hot" remedy to treat "cold" disorders, such as tiredness, lethargy, colds, catarrh, weak digestion, and tendency to infection.

• Cayenne used to be placed in woollen socks to warm the feet on cold winter days.

There are about 50 different species of plants called peppers, the main ones being black, white, and cayenne. Black and white pepper are the most popular of all the spices, and were the first to be brought to Europe from the Orient.

Internal

All three peppers have a warming, pungent taste and a stimulating effect that enhances the circulation and immune system. By increasing sweating and urination, they aid elimination of toxins and bring down fevers. They invigorate the digestive tract, improving the appetite and digestion, and, by stimulating digestive "fire", they enable the body to make full use of the nutrients it receives, and also ensure healthy elimination of toxins via the bowels. Black and white pepper contain piperine, which is similar in composition to morphine and an effective painkiller; cayenne owes its pungency to the alkaloid capsaicin. Cayenne is marvellous for the lungs as an expectorant, and its decongestant action relieves stuffiness and catarrh in the head and sinuses. Research has indicated that cayenne reduces the tendency to blood clots and lowers cholesterol. Cayenne is a warming and invigorating tonic, used for tiredness, nervous debility, and cold conditions. The burning sensation on the tongue tells the brain to secrete endorphins (natural opiates) which block pain and induce a feeling of well-being, sometimes even euphoria.

External

The three peppers act as rubefacients and counter-irritants, bringing inflammation to the surface and relieving pain. They can be added to liniments for nerve pain and painful joints, to gargles for sore throats, or used as an antiseptic for both cuts and wounds.

Black and white pepper come from the same shrub, a perennial climbing vine from the East and West Indies. Black pepper is made from dried, unripe peppercorns, while white is made from ripened peppercorns which have been soaked and their dark outer skins removed. Keep peppercorns whole and grind only when required, as pepper quickly loses its pungency. Cayenne is indigenous to Zanzibar, Mexico, and South America, and now grows in most tropical countries. Its name comes from the Greek meaning "to bite" – a reference to its pungent taste and properties.

VINEGAR

A Weak Acid with Strong Healing Powers

Properties

Antiseptic • Astringent • Diuretic • Antifungal • Decongestant

Folk remedies from the past
Hippocrates recommended vinegar for decongesting the respiratory system and to treat coughs.

• Rose petals soaked in vinegar is a Greek remedy for applying to sunburn and heat rash.

• Vinegar was once used as a dressing for wounds and when, in the old nursery rhyme, Jack fell down and broke his crown, he went to bed and wrapped his head in vinegar and brown paper!

• In the past, vinegar was taken diluted with water, as an antiseptic in typhus, dysentery, and scarlet fever. Mixed with salt it made an excellent emetic for clearing infections and poisons quickly from the system.

Add a dash of vinegar to dried beans when they are nearly cooked to render them less wind-producing.

Vinegar is widely used as a preservative and a condiment, and its acidic nature has made it a potent remedy dating back thousands of years.

Internal

Vinegar's acidity inhibits bacteria so it makes a good antiseptic in the gut as well as in the urinary system where it has been used for infections such as cystitis. A teaspoonful of vinegar in a glass of water sipped frequently makes a cooling remedy for fevers and infections, a decongestant for catarrh in the head and chest, and an excellent gargle to ease sore throats and laryngitis. Apple cider vinegar, a remedy originally made famous by Dr. Jarvis of Vermont, USA, is prescribed for a host of ailments, including digestive problems, asthma and hay fever, measles, sinusitis, and anxiety. Apples are highly nutritious, so cider vinegar is also given to correct mineral deficiencies and as a general tonic. In addition, this vinegar improves the breakdown and absorption of calcium and so is particularly recommended for strengthening teeth and nails, for arthritis, and osteoporosis. Taken with honey, cider vinegar has been prescribed for stomach ulcers, colitis, high blood pressure, bowel infections, and insomnia.

External

Vinegar acts as an astringent, checking bleeding, and reducing inflammation and swelling. It can be applied to bruises, sprains, strains, rashes, and insect stings. Bathe with a little vinegar added to the bath to calm skin irritations and conditions such as eczema. Sponged on to the skin, vinegar has a cooling effect, relieving sunburn and feverish headaches. The antifungal properties of vinegar make it a good treatment for ringworm and athlete's foot.

MUSTARD

A Tasty Condiment to Enhance Digestion and Dispel Infection

Properties

Stimulant • Antibacterial • Antifungal • Emetic • Rubefacient

Most of us know mustard as a condiment, which usually consists of a mixture of mustard seeds, wheat flour, turmeric, vinegar, and other spices. Mustard has been used in this way probably since the Romans brought it to England to enhance the flavour of meat. In 1623, Gerard said: "seed of mustard pounded with vinegar is an excellent sauce, good to be eaten with any goose meates, either fish or flesh, because it doth help digestion, warmeth the stomach and provoketh appetite." Its Latin name, *Sinapis*, refers to the "sinapisms", or hot mustard plasters, that were applied externally near the seat of internal inflammation, to relieve congestion of the underlying organs by drawing blood to the surface. They were used for rheumatism, arthritis, gout, and neuralgia.

Internal

The stimulating properties of mustard can be put to good use in winter to ward off the effects of cold, poor circulation, chilblains, lethargy, colds, flu, and depression. Mustard also stimulates digestion and enhances absorption. Black mustard seeds are more pungent than white, but be careful not to eat too much of either, as they can irritate the stomach lining, especially if you have an acid stomach or ulcers. The volatile oils in mustard have antimicrobial properties – you can use an infusion of ground mustard seeds for chest infections, colds and flu, rheumatism, and arthritis.

External

Mustard's volatile oils have a rubefacient (counter-irritant) effect, bringing blood to the skin in contact with it. A hot foot bath draws blood to the feet and relieves congestion in the head or lungs. An infusion makes an effective antiseptic gargle for sore throats and tonsillitis.

Folk remedies from the past

White and black mustard seeds have been used as medicines since the earliest times. Hippocrates recommended white mustard internally for digestive disorders and externally, mixed with vinegar, to draw out inflammation.

• White mustard seeds contain mucilage and were once fashionable as a laxative, especially for chronic constipation. When infused in hot water they were used as a cure for hiccoughs.

• The irritant effect of mustard provided a wonderful folk remedy for poisoning – 1 teaspoonful in a cup of hot water drunk all at once would provoke vomiting.

• In Russia, a daily dusting of mustard in woollen socks was thought to keep colds at bay.

CAUTION

Only use mustard seeds or powder, as mustard oil is toxic, especially if it is undiluted.

APPLE

"An Apple a Day Keeps the Doctor Away"

Properties

Digestive • Nutritious • Antiviral • Lowers cholesterol • Detoxifying • Laxative

Folk remedies from the past

Apples' medicinal virtues have been recorded since the days of the ancient Greeks and Romans. In Greek mythology the apple tasted like honey and healed all ailments.

- In folk medicine apples were used to treat: flu, fevers, bronchial complaints, heart problems, lethargy, and anaemia; to decongest the nose and chest of mucus; and to speed recovery during convalescence. All this seems to confirm the old saying: "To eat an apple going to bed, will make a doctor beg his bread."
- Cooked apples were valued as a sedative to calm anxiety and promote restful sleep.
- Grated raw apple was used as a poultice for bruised or sore eyes and applied to varicose ulcers.

The apple is a storehouse of vitamins, minerals, and other vital nutrients that are easily digested. It also dampens the appetite – a great bonus if you are dieting.

Internal

The apple is a wonderful aid to digestion. Its malic and tartaric acids regulate stomach acidity and help digestion of protein and fat which is why it has traditionally been eaten with pork and goose. It is a wonderful detoxifying remedy, promoting liver function and urination, and aiding the elimination of uric acid. These qualities explain why the apple can be helpful for liver and gall-bladder problems, indigestion, hyperacidity, gastritis, peptic ulcers, irritable bowel syndrome, arthritis, gout, fluid retention, urinary stones, and headaches. Apple's laxative properties are due to its pectin, which helps to bulk out stools, but apple can also help diarrhoea. Grated apple has been used for infantile diarrhoea, particularly when due to teething, and it is also reputed to relieve dysentery and colitis. Modern research has revealed that the apple and its juice are potent enemies of viruses; those who eat more apples tend to suffer fewer colds and upper respiratory infections. Eating two or three apples a day can also significantly lower blood cholesterol (particularly in women) and reduce blood pressure. They can also help diabetics by regulating blood sugar.

External

Baked apples were used for a variety of complaints. They were applied for earache; mashed with a little sulphur and applied to the skin for scabies and ringworm; and mixed with equal quantities of olive oil for use on lingering wounds.

Modern research has revealed that apples have significant antiviral properties. Their tannic acid is particularly active against the herpes simplex virus. Other constituents in apples, called polyphenols, have anti-cancer properties, and the pectin is able to bind to toxic metals, such as mercury and lead, and carry them out of the body. So, the apple is well equipped to protect against some of the effects of modern pollution, as well as age-old ailments.

ALCOHOL

Warming, Relaxing, and Definitely Beneficial – in Small Doses!

Properties

Relaxant • Vasodilator • Appetizer • Depressant • Antiseptic • Diuretic

Folk remedies from the past

Wine was well known to the ancient Egyptians, as their drawings and carvings reveal.

• The ancient Greeks not only drank wine, they used it as an antiseptic to cleanse wounds on the battlefield. It was also said to cleanse the bowels, cure constipation and insomnia, kill worms, and clear urinary problems.

• Drink has traditionally been used for solace, for "drowning one's sorrows". According to Homer, when Patroclus, the friend of Achilles, was killed in the Trojan Wars, Achilles wept for three days, after which he ate and drank for solace.

• The anaesthetic qualities of alcohol were used for dulling pain in the early days of operations and tooth extractions.

A hot whisky or brandy toddy, taken before bed, will induce sweating and help to bring down a fever and throw off infection.

CAUTION

Avoid wine if you are pregnant, or if you suffer from migraine or gout.

"Drink a glass of wine after your soup and you steal a rouble from your doctor" says an old Russian proverb. Wine was first made some 10,000 years ago, and it has a long association with religious festivals, perhaps due to the euphoria it produces and its association with fruitfulness. Its ability to dissolve many substances has made it invaluable in preparing medicines. As an antiseptic, it has been useful against cholera and typhoid.

Internal

Alcohol acts primarily on the nervous system, both as a depressant and relaxant. It delays and diminishes nervous responses to stimuli, and reduces inhibitions, leading to enlivened behaviour. It relaxes the digestive tract, relieving tension and spasm, and enhancing appetite, digestion, and absorption at the same time. The warming effects of alcohol are felt at once, bringing a flushed look to the face, and a sense of warmth and well-being. Recent research has shown that small amounts of red wine, taken regularly, inactivate viruses and bacteria. The polyphenols responsible also act as potent antioxidants, mopping up the free radicals which cause cell destruction. Regular drinking of alcohol has been linked to liver degeneration, higher rates of certain cancers, and high blood pressure. However, tests have shown that a half pint of beer or cider, or a glass of wine a day lowers cholesterol and helps prevent arterial and heart disease.

External

Apply alcohol to wounds as an astringent to stop bleeding and prevent infection. It speeds repair and relieves pain. Alcohol also hardens the skin, and can be applied to bed sores and sore nipples. A liniment acts as a counter-irritant for gout, rheumatism, and arthritis.

WHEAT

A Well-balanced and Nutritious Food – the Staff of Life

Properties

Laxative • Diuretic • Antioxidant • Tonic • Anti-ageing

Wheat is the most widely consumed grain in the US and Europe, mainly because it makes the best bread. As a food, whole wheat is highly nutritious, although not everyone can tolerate it – it is implicated in several allergies. Its nutrient value varies according to the health of the soil.

Internal

Wheat has been used in the past as a remedy for many ailments, including loss of appetite, weakness and debility, nutritional deficiencies, and anaemia. It was given as an expectorant for chest infections, as a diuretic for fluid retention, and as a remedy for gall stones. Two components of wheat deserve special mention: bran and wheatgerm. By treating and preventing constipation, bran helps to prevent diverticular disease, hiatus hernia, haemorrhoids, and varicose veins. There is now no doubt that bran also reduces the incidence of bowel cancer by diluting carcinogens and speeding their elimination from the bowel. Wheatgerm is rich in vitamin E, an important antioxidant, which protects cells from the harmful effects of free radicals. It is thought to slow down the ageing process, keeping the skin young-looking, to benefit the heart and circulation, and to protect the lungs against pollution. It can help relieve PMT and menopausal symptoms, and may enhance fertility, helping to ensure a healthy pregnancy and childbirth.

External

If you have oily skin, try scrubbing your face with bran; mixed with egg white it can be used instead of soap and will help prevent large pores. A hot bread and milk poultice will bring boils and abscesses to a head, and also draw out thorns and splinters. Wheatgerm oil has been used to speed the healing of burns and scars, and to prevent stretch marks during pregnancy.

Folk remedies from the past

Humanity has a long association with wheat; it was first cultivated in Mesopotamia some 10,000 years ago. Hippocrates prescribed it as a laxative.

• In Ayurveda, the ancient medical tradition of India, wheat is a "kapha" food, very suitable for growing children.

• A Russian remedy for a head cold involves burning a piece of bread slowly and inhaling for 2-3 minutes at a time.

• Burnt bread has been recommended to clear the system of toxins and so help to clear the skin.

Bran tea is a treatment for sore throats. Boil 2 tablespoons of bran in 600ml (1 pint) of water for 20 minutes. Add 1 tablespoon of honey and 7g (0.25oz) gum arabic, and stir. Strain through muslin and drink.

EGG

A Valuable Food – Nutritious and Easily Digested

Properties

Body-building • Demulcent • Poison antidote

Folk remedies from the past

- In Russia, a burn was treated by applying raw scrambled egg and then pouring alcohol slowly over it, to form a protective film.
- A beaten egg white was an old remedy for relieving bruises, sprains, and whitlows.
- Eggs were said to relieve nerve pain and inflammation as in neuralgia and sciatica.
- In the 1920s and '30s, doctors used egg yolk preparations to treat infant diarrhoea, due to the egg's binding properties.

Eggs are highly nutritious – a fact that is hardly surprising given that a chick lives on its contents until it is hatched. An egg must therefore contain the necessary nutrients for body building, such as first-class proteins, fats, and valuable minerals, but not carbohydrates. Its nutrients include phosphorus, calcium, iron, sodium, potassium, magnesium, zinc, vitamins A, B complex, C, D, E, and folic acid.

Internal

Eggs are easily digested and so make a valuable food for children, the elderly, and convalescents. Raw and lightly boiled eggs (in the days before salmonella) were considered a strengthening tonic and ideal food for invalids, particularly those with tuberculosis and anaemia. The egg white acts as a demulcent, soothing inflammation of the mucous membranes of the stomach and bowel that causes heartburn, indigestion, diarrhoea, or constipation. Egg white, beaten in milk, is also a first-aid antidote to corrosive poisons. Despite their nutritious value, however, eggs are a common offending food in a wide range of childhood allergies.

External

Eggs are soothing to the skin. To relieve the soreness of sunburn, nappy rash, or cracked nipples, apply egg white in layers, allowing each layer to dry. For burns, beat an egg white until stiff and spread on the affected area, or, for even greater effect, add three tablespoons of olive oil to the white before whisking. Eggs have been used as a protein hair conditioner and many shampoos contain egg for this reason. To check hair fall, try rubbing beaten fresh eggs mixed with water into your scalp and leaving overnight, before washing the next morning.

For abscesses, beat a fresh egg with 3 tablespoons of white flour and cook to a thick paste in a bain-marie. Spread on gauze and bandage to the affected area, repeating every 3 hours.

CAUTION

Due to contamination by salmonella in recent years, eggs should be avoided by pregnant women, the sick, and the elderly.

Eggs are high in protein and fat: the white consists chiefly of the protein ovo-albumin, while the yolk contains proteins and fatty materials, including lipids such as lecithin, and cholesterol. Because of the high cholesterol, many people have drastically reduced the number of eggs in their diet. However, lecithin (also a natural component of beans and peas) has the special property of being able to dissolve cholesterol and other fats. Research in the US has recently shown that eggs laid by birds in daylight are lower in cholesterol than those laid by battery hens.

MILK AND YOGHURT

A Great Restorative Remedy

Properties

Body-building • Restorative • Soothing • Antifungal • Possibly anticarcinogenic

Folk remedies from the past
In many cultures, milk is a symbol of sacrifice, of willingness to put others' needs before one's own – hence "the milk of human kindness".

• In India, where dairying is important, the family cow is treated with great respect.

• Bulgarians were once renowned for living longer – and because they ate large amounts of yoghurt, their longevity was attributed to this food.

• Yoghurt's ability to ward off diarrhoea and bowel problems has been known for centuries.

• To keep their skin clear, soft, and supple, people were recommended to sponge their body with a litre (1.75 pints) of milk mixed with the juice of 2 lemons.

Yoghurt is very useful in the treatment of yeast infections such as thrush. Plain live yoghurt applied to the affected area 2–3 times daily will relieve itching and clear the infection quickly.

Human milk is unique in that it contains everything in the correct proportions that a human requires for normal health and development. Cows' milk is a rich source of nutrients and was considered an ideal restorative food for those who were run down and debilitated, and was given to the chronically sick, old, and infirm. Yoghurt is sour fermented milk curdled by bacteria, which confer a wide range of health-giving properties, helping to protect against heart disease, bowel infection, and possibly cancer.

Internal

Cows' milk is geared more to the development of bones and flesh than to the brain and nervous system while mother's milk is the opposite; and, unlike human milk, it encourages bacterial growth in the intestine. Its alkalinity depresses the digestion of protein, and the presence of lactose may give rise to a variety of allergies and digestive problems. Milk also has a tendency to increase mucus production, which may exacerbate catarrhal diseases. However, it is a good remedy to prevent osteoporosis if drunk during childhood, and its soothing, alkaline properties can ease indigestion. Many people who find they cannot tolerate milk eat yoghurt instead, which is equally nutritious. Live yoghurt is the best medicine for re-establishing a normal bacterial population in the gut after a course of antibiotics.

External

Milk is soothing when applied to the skin. It is used in many beauty preparations such as cleansing milks, combined with, for example, honey or chamomile. Buttermilk or yoghurt compresses will relieve the heat and soreness of sunburn.

CABBAGE

The Poor Man's Medicine Chest

Properties

Detoxifying • Diuretic • Anti-inflammatory • Tonic • Antiseptic

Cabbage is an extremely valuable food source when eaten raw or lightly steamed. It contains vitamins A, B, C, and E, as well as minerals including calcium, sulphur, silica, magnesium, and iodine. It is rich in iron and chlorophyll, making it an excellent remedy for anaemia, and has been used as a nutritive tonic to restore strength in debility and convalescence. It is said to replenish the blood in those who feel run down.

Internal

Cabbage has been the subject of a great deal of research, much of which confirms its ancient uses. It stimulates the immune system and antibody production and, taken as a soup or tea, is a wonderful way to ward off infections such as colds, coughs, and flu. Its sulphur compounds may confer its antiseptic action in the respiratory system. Cabbage also has an amazing ability to heal ulcers, both internal and external. Eaten raw, it coats the lining of the digestive tract with protective mucilaginous substances and helps relieve peptic ulcers, gastritis, heartburn, and ulcerative colitis. A regular intake of cabbage prevents constipation, lowers the risk of cancer, particularly of the colon, and benefits the liver. It may also reduce blood sugar, helping diabetics.

External

Cabbage leaves are soothing, antiseptic, and healing, and draw out toxins from the skin. A poultice will bring relief to wounds, burns, boils, bruises, ulcers, blisters, stings, cold sores, shingles, headaches, and neuralgia, and also acts as an anti-inflammatory for swollen joints. Applied to the chest it soothes a harsh cough, and applied to the lower abdomen it soothes cystitis and renal colic, and relieves fluid retention. Cabbage juice is good for burns, bites, cold sores, acne, and impetigo.

Folk remedies from the past

Cabbage is one of the most highly esteemed remedies in medicinal folklore. The early Egyptians so revered it that they built a temple in its honour, while in ancient Rome cabbage was regarded as a cure-all. Cato the Censor said that it was thanks to cabbage that the Romans lived for six centuries without physicians.

• Pythagoras recommended a daily diet of raw cabbage to cure nervous disorders. It was used by sailors to prevent scurvy.

• Raw cabbage was reputed to purify the blood and clear the skin, detoxify the liver, cure arthritis, headaches, and hangovers, and even dry out alcoholics.

You can make a cabbage leaf poultice by discarding the ribs from the greenest leaves, warming them in hot water, and then crushing them with a rolling pin. Apply several layers and hold in place with a bandage or cling film, changing it every few hours.

TEA

The Divine Leaf

Properties

Stimulant • Diuretic • Astringent • Antioxidant

Folk remedies from the past

For more than 4000 years, tea has been used as a medicine in China. The ancient Greeks called it "the divine leaf" and prescribed it for asthma, colds, and bronchitis.

- The application of cold tea is an old remedy for burns and scalds, as well as swollen eyes.
- Powdered tea was once used as a snuff to stop nose bleeds.

CAUTION

Too much tea over a long period can be a bad thing. It may cause anxiety, insomnia, panic attacks, depression, migraine, PMS, headaches, tremors, and abnormal heart patterns. Tea is not recommended for those with gastritis or stomach ulcers since it stimulates the production of gastric juices in the stomach. It also contributes to constipation, particularly in the elderly, wind, indigestion, and can inhibit absorption of iron and zinc – worth noting by women of child-bearing age or those who are pregnant.

The two major kinds of tea, black and green, come from the same plant and contain several alkaloids, including caffeine, theobromine, and xanthine – all of which have similar stimulating effects. A cup of tea has about 50mg of caffeine, which stimulates your nervous system, improves reflexes, decreases fatigue, and brings a feeling of well-being.

Internal

Tea stimulates those parts of the nervous system which regulate breathing, digestion, and blood circulation. It relieves constriction in the bronchial tubes which occurs in asthma. The heart beat is also quickened, and peripheral blood vessels are dilated, causing less blood to flow to the abdominal area and more to the brain and kidneys. The increased flow to the kidneys in turn increases urine output. Tea's high tannin content protects mucous membranes from irritation, reduces catarrh, and checks bleeding, making it a good remedy for sinusitis and diarrhoea. Research suggests that tannins may inhibit bacterial and viral infections, such as flu, herpes, and polio. Research in Japan indicates that green tea can block certain cancers from forming and habitual green tea drinkers are reported to have lower rates of stomach cancer. Tea's catchins may retard the furring up of arteries, and have antioxidant effects which help protect against heart disease and cancer, and slow the ageing process.

External

For cuts and wounds, tea's astringent effect checks bleeding and guards against infection. Cold tea makes a good healing lotion for sores and ulcers, and can be used as a mouthwash for ulcers and bleeding gums. The natural fluorine in tea helps reduce tooth cavities.

According to Chinese legend, tea was discovered by the Emperor Shen-Nung in 2737 BC*. Another story tells how tea was introduced into China by an Indian ascetic. Whatever is origins, tea has become one of the world's most popular drinks. In some Asian countries, tea drinking has evolved into a delicate art where water, brewing conditions, and utensils are carefully monitored by connoisseurs. The famous Japanese Tea Ceremony is a time-honoured institution rooted in Zen Buddhism and founded on the idea of the adoration of the beautiful in the daily routine of life.*

BARLEY

The Food of the Gladiators!

Properties

Nutritious • Soothing • Strengthening • Tonic

Folk remedies from the past

Physicians of ancient Greece used barley to enhance vitality and treat inflamed conditions of the digestive system. Roman gladiators were called hordearii – barley eaters – because they ate barley to build up strength.

- Cows' milk was diluted with barley to prevent the formation of hard curds in the stomach.
- Eating sprouted barley helps to dry mother's milk when weaning and to relieve painful, swollen breasts.

To make barley water, boil 1 heaped teaspoon of barley in 1 litre (1.75 pints) of water for half an hour, then strain off the liquid.

For thousands of years, people in the Near East have grown barley. Barley is both easily digested and highly nutritious; it is rich in calcium, potassium, protein, and vitamins B and E. Barley has a reputation as a strengthening nerve tonic, relieving stress and fatigue. The best way to retain both the nutritional and medical benefits of barley is to use the whole grain.

Internal

Barley promotes the normal functioning of the heart and stabilizes blood pressure. The outer husk is rich in chemicals which inhibit the synthesis of cholesterol by the liver, while substances inside the grain further reduce cholesterol. Research suggests that barley contains chemicals called protease inhibitors which suppress cancer-causing agents in the digestive tract. Barley's wonderfully soothing properties relieve inflammation in the digestive, respiratory, and urinary systems. It improves digestion and appetite, promotes liver function, and makes an excellent remedy for children with digestive upsets and intestinal disturbances caused by candida. Barley water, soup, and gruel have been used to combat wind, colic, diarrhoea, and constipation, and were traditionally used in the sick room to build up a patient's strength. Barley water moistens the lungs, relieves a sore chest, and eases dry and tickly coughs. Gargle the water to relieve a sore throat, and sweeten with honey when giving to children. Barley water makes an excellent remedy for soothing cystitis when taken frequently through the day.

External

A poultice of barley flour may be applied to soothe inflammations of the skin.

CLOVE

Warming, Pungent, and Stimulating!

Properties

Antimicrobial • Expectorant • Carminative • Astringent
Anaesthetic • Antidepressant

Said to be the most stimulating of the aromatic spices, clove has a pungent, warming effect that increases "fire" in the stomach, allays nausea, soothes indigestion and hiccoughs, stimulates the circulation, and enhances liver function. It is also a powerful antiseptic, and is used for infections of the digestive, respiratory, and urinary systems (whether bacterial, viral, or fungal) and in many oral hygiene products.

Internal

Those who suffer from the cold will feel a warm glow all over after drinking clove tea or wine mulled with cloves. It is a wonderful remedy for the nervous system, relaxing tension, relieving anxiety, and lifting depression. In the respiratory system it serves as an expectorant to clear phlegm and helps ward off colds and other infections, while its warmth induces sweating and can help bring down a fever. Hay fever and rhinitis sufferers may find relief in the antihistamine action of clove tea. As an aid to digestion, cloves reduce spasm, relieve wind, and enhance absorption, while the astringent qualities of the tannins are useful in treating diarrhoea. Eaten in the few weeks before childbirth, cloves prime the uterus for contraction, and clove oil has been used as a massage for sluggish contractions, during the birth.

External

If you have a headache, try inhaling clove oil or rubbing it on to your temples. Its anaesthetic properties will also deaden the pain of toothache – simply apply a piece of oil-soaked cotton wool to the offending tooth. By adding clove oil to dilute alcohol, you can concoct a liniment to relieve aching muscles and arthritis. It is a useful healing disinfectant for cuts and wounds, and for treating ringworm and athlete's foot.

Folk remedies from the past

The oldest recorded medicinal use of clove was in China, where it was used for a variety of ailments, including diarrhoea and hernia, as early as 240 BC. In the courts of China it was used to sweeten the breath and it was customary for cloves to be held in the mouth during audiences with the Emperor.

• In Elizabethan days, pomanders were made by studding oranges with cloves and letting them dry out. They were then hung from ribbons in wardrobes for their wonderful aroma and to repel moths, and carried about to counteract bad odours and disease-carrying germs.

To aid digestion, particularly after a heavy meal, make a delicious tea by simmering a mixture of cloves, cinnamon, and ginger for 15 minutes.

CAUTION

Do not use during pregnancy.

CARROT

Humble Vegetable or Panacea?

Properties

Nutritious • Expectorant • Antiseptic • Antioxidant • Diuretic

Folk remedies from the past

Carrots were first mentioned in writings by the ancient Greeks 2500 years ago. Hippocrates used carrots in his remedies in 430 BC.

• Carrots have been used as a remedy for tuberculosis, scrofula, bronchitis, and pneumonia. A decoction of carrot seeds was taken for dysentery.

• A vital Russian folk remedy was fresh carrot juice with honey and a little water. It was taken daily by the tablespoonful to cure colds and coughs and ward off winter-time respiratory ailments.

• Carrots are said to regulate women's menstrual flow and enhance milk production.

Make carrot soup by boiling 0.5kg (1lb) of fresh carrots in 1 litre (1.75 pints) water until soft, and then blend.

Carrots are an excellent restorative food if you are feeling run down or convalescing, and for correcting nutritional deficiency, such as anaemia, and keeping tooth decay at bay. Highly nutritious, carrots are rich in vitamins A, B, and C, beta carotene, and in iron, calcium, potassium, and sodium.

Internal

Carrots have long been associated with sharp eyesight, but are also famed for regulating intestinal activity and relieving constipation and diarrhoea. Carrots stimulate the appetite and can relieve wind, colic, intestinal infections, peptic ulcers, and haemorrhoids. A carrot juice fast for one or two days is a great detoxifying therapy for the liver. Carrots' diuretic effect relieves fluid retention and soothes cystitis. They help counter the formation of kidney stones, and relieve arthritis and gout. Their expectorant properties help expel mucus from the chest in coughs, bronchitis, and asthma, while the antiseptic effect helps resolve infections. Research has confirmed carrots' folk use as a circulatory remedy, protecting against arterial and heart disease, preventing hardening of the arteries, and increasing haemoglobin and red blood cell counts. Eating two or three medium-sized carrots a day can lower blood cholesterol by more than 10 per cent. Beta carotene has been shown to inhibit cancer, particularly that related to smoking, and the antioxidants help to slow ageing.

External

You can use grated raw carrot in a poultice, as an antiseptic, and to speed healing of wounds, varicose ulcers, burns, whitlows, boils, abscesses, and styes. Carrot broth can heal chilblains and chapped skin, soothe itching from eczema, and treat impetigo and cold sores.

Not only are carrots believed to help you see in the dark, they are also valued for their digestive properties, having been described as "great friends of the intestine". Their Latin name, Daucus, *comes from the Greek "daio", meaning to burn, due to their pungent and stimulating qualities, which are particularly noticeable in the seeds. They have a wonderful cleansing effect on the liver and digestive system, and can help to clear skin problems. In 1960, scientists isolated an ingredient in carrots called daucarine, capable of dilating blood vessels and so protecting against arterial and heart disease.*

OLIVE OIL

A Symbol of Peace and Purity

Properties

Laxative • Anti-inflammatory • Vasodilator • Demulcent
Anticarcinogenic • Anti-ageing

Folk remedies from the past

To the Greeks, olives are a symbol of wisdom. It is said that the goddess Athena won an island from Poseidon by presenting its inhabitants with the gift which would be of greatest value to them – the olive tree.

• An enema of warm olive oil was a common remedy to relieve constipation, as it helps to break up faeces.

• A traditional remedy for a sluggish liver and gall bladder problems was a tablespoonful of cold pressed oil taken first thing in the morning to stimulate the flow of bile into the intestines.

• Children who wet the bed used to be massaged over their kidneys with warm oil.

Try olive leaf tea to reduce a fever. Soak 30g (1oz) of leaves in 600ml (1 pint) of cold water for 6–8 hours. Bring to the boil and then leave to infuse for 30 minutes. Drink freely.

Since olives were first cultivated some 6000 years ago, they have been highly valued for cooking, medicinal, and cosmetic purposes. The pale greenish yellow oil is highly nutritious and believed to be the purest of all vegetable fats – so pure, in fact, that it was used to provide extra nourishment for babies by rubbing it into their skin. In the Bible, the olive tree represented peace and goodwill as well as life and hope.

Internal

The sweet, fruity-tasting oil is highly mucilaginous, and its demulcent properties have long been used to treat a variety of digestive problems, including wind, indigestion, heartburn, gastritis and peptic ulcers, colitis and constipation, and respiratory problems, particularly harsh dry coughs, laryngitis, croup, and catarrh. Those whose diet is high in olive oil can expect to live longer, for scientists have shown how the oil reduces harmful cholesterol levels and the tendency to atherosclerosis, heart attacks, and strokes. It also helps to lower blood pressure and the risk of blood clots. Olive oil may counteract the spread of cancer and retard the ageing process through the action of its antioxidants.

External

Use olive oil to protect your skin from irritation and make it more supple, to soothe eczema, chapped skin, and cold sores, and to soften crusts of cradle cap in babies. Try dropping some warm oil into your ear to soften accumulated ear wax, or use the oil as a vehicle for other oils (garlic or lavender) to relieve the pain of earache. Olive oil with grated garlic makes an excellent liniment for joint pains, neuralgia, and sprains, while an infusion of the leaves can be used for cleaning cuts, or as a mouthwash for bleeding gums.

WATER

Called the Greatest of All Healers

Properties

Cleansing • Circulatory stimulant • Relaxant • Invigorating • Detoxifying

Water composes the major proportion of all living things, including the human body. The right water balance in the body is essential for the healthy circulation of blood, the function of every cell in the body, and the maintenance of correct osmotic pressure and electrolyte balance.

Internal

Water in food and drink is necessary to bulk out stools and prevent constipation, and to flush wastes and toxins out through the skin and urinary system. Plenty of water to drink is vital during a fever, or in diarrhoea and vomiting, to prevent dehydration. After a heavy drinking session, flush your system with as much water as possible to avoid a hangover. Hot water sipped slowly will often relieve hiccoughs, indigestion, and wind, and a drink of water when feeling faint can act as a stimulant to the heart. "Hard" water, containing dissolved calcium and magnesium salts, may protect against heart disease.

External

Bathing in varying temperatures of water, fresh or salt, is a stimulating experience for the whole body, improving the function of the skin and helping it to eliminate wastes via the pores. Cold baths stimulate the lungs and circulation, increase vitality, enhance resistance to infection by increasing the white blood cell count, and even aid fertility by raising sex hormone levels. Tepid baths, on the other hand, are used therapeutically for 30 minutes to raise low blood pressure and calm nerves. Warm baths relieve muscle tension, aching, and cystitis, and are very relaxing and restoring. Avoid over-hot baths as they stress the heart and increase the pulse. Steam, however, when inhaled, is excellent for sore throats and laryngitis, and is often the best cure for croup.

Folk remedies from the past

The custom of bathing, both for cleansing and for health benefits, dates from very early times. Bathrooms have been discovered among the ruins of ancient Egypt, and in Greece they date from around 1500 BC. The Romans, renowned for their love of luxury, had hot water, steam, and cold baths, and used them as social centres for meeting friends and doing business.

• Around 1800, hydrotherapy was established in Europe for treating health problems.

• Charles Darwin remarked that a cold dip made his aches and pains disappear – later studies have confirmed that a short sharp shock benefits the immune system and circulation of the blood..

A good way to wake yourself up in the morning is to take a cold bath. Then dry yourself vigorously and dress quickly, and you should feel a warm afterglow. Not recommended for the sick, old, or very young.

GARLIC

Drives Away Infections – As Well As Vampires!

Properties

Antiseptic • Decongestant • Antioxidant • Hypotensive • Circulatory stimulant
Digestive • Anthelmintic • Febrifuge

Folk remedies from the past

An Egyptian medical papyrus from 1500 BC includes more than 200 prescriptions using garlic for problems such as headaches, weakness, and throat infections.

• At the beginning of the 20th century garlic preparations were still a major remedy for TB and during World War I it was used to combat dysentery and typhus.

• Garlic has long been known as an invigorating tonic and used in many "elixirs of youth". Street vendors in 5th century BC Greece apparently sold garlic with the chant "It is the truth, garlic gives men youth".

The humble garlic bulb, much maligned for its lingering odour, is an ancient remedy with a powerful effect on infections. When crushed, raw garlic releases allicin which is strongly antibiotic. After circulating in the blood stream, allicin is excreted via the lungs, bowels, skin, and urinary system – all of which are disinfected in the process.

Internal

Garlic's antimicrobial effect can help to combat sore throats, colds and flu, bronchial and lung infections, as well as infections in the gut, candidiasis, and worms. In the respiratory system, garlic also acts as a decongestant and expectorant, making it an excellent remedy for coughs, chest infections, and bronchial asthma. Because it causes sweating, it can be used to bring down a fever. Garlic improves digestion, stimulating the secretion of digestive juices and the movement of food through the gut. Its antiseptic action cleanses the liver and the digestive system, thereby improving general health. Research has shown garlic's ability to lower blood sugar and cholesterol significantly, and to reduce blood pressure and a tendency to clotting. Research also shows that garlic acts as a powerful antioxidant and its sulphur compounds can inhibit tumours.

External

Garlic may be crushed, macerated in oil, or made into an ointment and applied to cuts, inflamed joints, rheumatism, sprains, athlete's foot, ringworm, as well as stings and bites. An oil infusion can be dropped into the ear to relieve earache, and rubbed into the chest to treat coughs and chest infections, such as bronchitis and whooping cough.

To make garlic juice for coughs, colds, and sore throats: cut several cloves into thin pieces, cover with honey and leave for 2–3 hours. Take the extracted juice in teaspoonfuls frequently through the day.

Garlic has a most powerful effect on infections, being antibacterial, antifungal, antiparasitic, and antiviral. It has been used successfully in the past to treat food poisoning, diarrhoea and dysentery, cholera, and typhoid, and its antiseptic, cleansing action can work throughout the body. Perhaps garlic's ability to drive away infection is linked to its reputation for driving away vampires! In many traditions garlic was hung in strings from roofs of houses and sterns of boats to prevent attack by witches, sorcerers, demons, and evil spirits.

LEEK

Warming and Stimulating: A Tonic for the Whole Body

Properties

Expectorant • Diuretic • Relaxant • Laxative • Antiseptic
Digestive • Hypotensive

Folk remedies from the past
The Greeks and Romans used leeks as a remedy for coughs and to improve the voice. According to Pliny, the Roman emperor Nero ate only leeks and oil for certain days in the month to keep his throat healthy in preparation for his singing performances.

• Eating only boiled leeks was an old remedy for swallowing a sharp object such as a needle. The fibres were said to sheath the object and prevent it from damaging the stomach or bowel, until it was passed through the system.

A leek broth is easy to make and excellent for replacing minerals lost during sickness and diarrhoea. Simply simmer 8–10 leeks in 2–3 litres (3–5 pints) of water for 1–2 hours.

Syrup of leeks is an effective remedy for chest infections. Cook a few leeks in water and extract the juice by squeezing through a cloth when soft. Add honey and give regularly.

Not only do leeks make a delicious food, but they are also highly nutritious. They are rich in potassium, magnesium, silica, iron, and calcium, as well as vitamins C and B complex. Eaten regularly they provide an easily digested tonic to the whole system, and are recommended during convalescence.

Internal

Leeks were prized as an effective cough remedy. Their warming and stimulating properties, together with their expectorant action, help to clear congestion from the respiratory tract, providing relief for hoarseness, sore throats, colds, catarrh, and other chest infections. Their cleansing diuretic action and ability to eliminate uric acid from the body make them a valuable remedy for gout and arthritis, as well as urinary problems such as cystitis and urethritis. Like onions and garlic, they are powerfully antiseptic, and also help to protect the heart and arteries by preventing arteriosclerosis and high blood pressure. In the digestive tract they are warming and relaxing, and help to relieve inflammatory and infective conditions such as gastroenteritis and colitis. Leek broth helps to re-establish a normal bacterial population in the gut after antibiotics, and is a useful treatment for infant diarrhoea.

External

A poultice of leeks provides an antiseptic wound dressing, while a cut leek rubbed on to an insect sting can neutralize the poison and bring relief from pain. Apply a drawing paste of mashed cooked leeks on gauze to counter boils, abscesses, and whitlows. Leek broth, or leeks cooked in milk, make a soothing and healing lotion for inflamed skin and burns; this property has been known since the ancient Egyptians, who valued leeks highly for the treatment of burns.

CUCUMBER

A Cool and Light Food, Excellent for Hot Summer Days

Properties

Diuretic • Refrigerant • Anti-inflammatory • Depurative

The cooling and thirst-quenching properties of the cucumber have made it a popular food in hot countries for thousands of years: the Greeks and Romans were very fond of cucumbers, and in the Bible, the Israelites in the wilderness bemoaned the absence of them in their diet to Moses. In pharmacopoeias of the 18th century, cucumber seeds are noted as one of the four coldest seeds, used for cooling and to combat intestinal worms.

Internal

Although cucumbers consist of 95 per cent water, when unpeeled they are nourishing, containing vitamins A, B complex and C, and sulphur, manganese, phosphorus, calcium, and potassium. They are a light food and, due to their low calorific value, are good for slimmers. Their mild diuretic properties help weight loss where there is fluid retention, and also cleanse the system by increasing the elimination of toxins and wastes, including excess uric acid. This makes cucumber a good remedy for inflammatory arthritis and gout, as well as skin conditions such as eczema. In France, cooked cucumber is used to aid liver function and treat intestinal disorders and infections.

External

On the skin the cooling, soothing actions of cucumbers come into their own. They have long been famous in beauty treatments for keeping the skin young and free of wrinkles and blemishes. Apply cucumber juice to soothe inflamed skin conditions such as urticaria and eczema, to reduce pain and inflammation from cold sores and ant stings, and to cool sore and stinging eyes. Mixed equally with rosewater and glycerine, cucumber juice also eases sunburn and prickly heat. Cucumber water makes an ideal cleanser and toner for oily skins.

Folk remedies from the past

Cucumber has long been used wherever there is inflammation and heat in the system. In 1633, the herbalist Gerard said of cucumber that it "filleth the veines with naughty cold humours", and recommended it for inflamed chest and lung conditions, for excess heat in the stomach and bladder, for phlegm, and "copper red faces, red and shining fiery noses (as red as red roses) with pimples, pumples, rubies and such like precious faces."

• Cucumber is a cooling remedy for fevers – according to folklore, if a cucumber was placed alongside a sick child, then it would absorb the heat of the fever.

Collect cucumber juice by placing thin slices of peeled cucumber in a bowl for 2 hours and then filtering it through a fine cloth.

Make cucumber water by cutting a cucumber into cubes and boiling it in 2 pints (1 litre) of water for 15 minutes. Strain and press through a cloth.

ONION

Helps to Fight Infection and Heart Disease

Properties

Circulatory and digestive stimulant • Antiseptic • Detoxifying • Lowers cholesterol
Hypotensive • Hypoglycaemic • Diuretic

Folk remedies from the past

A close relation of garlic, the onion was deified by the ancient Egyptians as a cure-all and a symbol of vitality. It was used in religious rites and healing as early as 4000 BC, and as a prophylactic it has served against epidemics of infectious diseases such as cholera, and "the plague".

• Onions were used as an effective antiseptic for soldiers' wounds in World War II. A cut onion was traditionally placed in the sick room for its antiseptic vapours to cleanse the atmosphere.

• As an aphrodisiac, onion soup was customarily given to couples on their wedding night.

For all respiratory infections, prepare a juice of chopped raw onion drizzled with honey and leave overnight. Take by the dessertspoonful every 2 hours.

Traditionally, people have relied on onions to purify the blood and aid the heart and circulation. Modern research has shown that raw onions significantly lower bad LDL (low-density lipoprotein) cholesterol, helping to protect against heart attacks. Raw or cooked, onions reduce blood pressure, thin the blood, and dissolve blood clots.

Internal

Particularly when raw, onions are a pungent digestive stimulant and a good tonic for liver disorders, flatulence, and chronic constipation. They enhance digestion and absorption, acting as a nutritional energy tonic during convalescence and for tiredness, exhaustion, and anaemia. Onions are powerfully antiseptic, and will help ward off respiratory, gastrointestinal, and urinary tract infections. Their pungent effect increases circulation and causes sweating, helping to bring down fevers and sweat out colds and flu. Onions are excellent for sore throats, pharyngitis, rhinitis, colds, catarrh, sinusitis, breaking up mucus congestion, and as an expectorant for coughs and bronchitis. As a blood cleanser and diuretic, onions are good for water retention, urinary gravel, arthritis, and gout.

External

For wasp or bee stings, dab on a raw cut onion and place a slice on the sting. For warts, chop onions, cover with salt, and leave overnight. Dab the warts twice daily with the juice. You can also apply onion juice to burns, cuts, boils, abscesses, and animal bites; use it as drops for earache; and apply with cotton wool to ease toothache. Grated onion can be used as a poultice for chilblains and, when applied to the head and inhaled, to relieve headaches and migraine.

In modern folklore, onions are used throughout the world with incredible versatility. Onions are powerfully antiseptic, and research has confirmed their ability to fight many infecting bacteria, including salmonella. They have also been shown to lower cholesterol when half a medium raw onion is eaten each day. Research suggests that onion juice or cooked onion reduces blood sugar – confirming the folk use in diabetes – and investigations continue into the use of the sulphur compounds in onions as an anti-cancer remedy. Small wonder the ancients saw this miracle plant as a cure for all ailments.

CARDAMOM

A Warming Restorative to Generate Strength and Calm the Mind

Properties

Aromatic • Digestive • Tonic • Expectorant • Warming

Folk remedies from the past
Cardamom seeds originate from India where they are held in high esteem in Ayurvedic medicine for inducing a calm meditative state.

• Cardamom's tonic properties have been an important ingredient in European love potions. When used traditionally in aphrodisiac recipes it was often mixed with cinnamon, nutmeg, peppers, and onion.

• Ladies in 19th-century England carried cardamom seeds in their pockets. They chewed them for their digestive and tonic effects, and to sweeten the breath.

For a delicious warming tea, place 4 cardamom pods, 4 black peppercorns, 4 cloves, 1 cinnamon stick, and a few slices of fresh ginger in 600ml (1 pint) water. Heat – but do not boil – for half an hour and strain. Drink hot with a little milk or honey twice a day to ward off coughs and colds.

Cardamom's rich warm flavour and appetizing effects make it an excellent flavouring for drinks, desserts, relishes, liqueurs, and medicines. In India, the Middle East, Europe, and Latin America, this oil-bearing spice is an essential ingredient in curries, bread, cakes, and coffee.

Internal

Cardamom seeds have aromatic and warming properties, invigorating the stomach and intestines. They stimulate the appetite and enhance digestion. In a hot infusion they help relieve colic, distension, wind, nausea, vomiting, indigestion, and an acid stomach. Particularly valuable is their ability to reduce phlegm. You can add them to milk products and puddings to counteract milk's mucus-forming effects and aid its digestion. Cardamom seeds can be chewed after a meal to improve digestion and sweeten the breath; they help dispel the taste and smell of garlic and onion. Cardamom's expectorant action helps to expel phlegm from the chest in bronchial problems and clear nasal and sinus congestion. Cardamom has a wide reputation as a warming energy tonic; it is wonderfully restorative, particularly for dispelling the cold and damp effects of winter. It helps to generate strength, lift the spirits, calm anxiety, and allay lethargy and depression. The tonic action extends to the kidneys: it makes a strengthening remedy for incontinence and bed-wetting in children.

External

Use the diluted essential oil of cardamom for bruising, strains, and sprains, and as an antidote to poisons in insect bites and stings.

TURNIP

A Vegetable that Bestows Beauty and Health

Properties

Tonic • Decongestant • Bactericidal • Depurative • Diuretic

"Eat turnip and grow beautiful" goes an old saying, which may explain why people used to drink a cupful of boiled turnip green water first thing in the morning, to ensure bright eyes and a clear skin. Both the leaves and the root of this cruciferous plant have a long tradition of use in folk medicine, and are rich in vitamins and minerals. As the leaves in particular are high in calcium, iron, and copper, and vitamins A and C, they make an energy-giving tonic and blood purifier, useful for clearing skin problems. Turnips are low in carbohydrate, making them a good food for slimmers.

Internal

The turnip's reputation as a blood purifier is more than skin deep. It has a beneficial effect on the urinary system, aiding diuresis and the elimination of toxins, and was used traditionally for kidney stones (especially those composed of uric acid), gout, arthritis, fluid retention, and obesity. In Canada, the juice was taken to heal stomach ulcers, and the roots were eaten to treat bowel problems. Turnips have a bactericidal effect, particularly in the respiratory system. Research has shown that they enhance general immunity. Both the root and green tops are high in glucosinolates (especially when eaten raw) which are thought to block the development of cancer.

External

You can make a poultice for boils, abscesses, and chilblains out of crushed boiled turnips. Such a poultice is also soothing and healing to the skin. Try mashing the turnips with bread and milk for a particularly cleansing poultice – joints swollen from rheumatism, arthritis, and gout may also benefit from this remedy.

Folk remedies from the past

Traditionally, the whole turnip plant was used to combat scurvy and to correct nutritional deficiencies that cause weakness, lethargy, and low spirits.

• In France, a little raw turnip every day was recommended to clear skin problems, while the broth was used to treat lung diseases, colds, and a variety of respiratory infections.

• A purcc of turnips cooked in milk was a remedy for bronchitis, while the juice was given to treat TB.

• Such was the esteem in which turnips were held that they were used on armorial bearings to represent a person of liberal disposition who relieved the poor.

Turnip juice administered by the teaspoonful through the day is an effective decongestant, particularly for children's colds, coughs and catarrh. To make the juice, slice up a turnip, cover it with sugar, and leave for 2–3 hours.

FROM THE

GARDEN & HEDGEROW

Where the herbs are gathered together like kings in an assembly, there the doctor is called a sage, who destroys evil, and averts disease.

Rig Veda X.97 (Hymn to the Plants)

1. Of leaves, choose such only as are green, and full of juice; pick them carefully, and cast away such as are any way declining, for they will putrify the rest. So shall one handful be worth ten of those you buy in any of the shops.

2. Note what places they most delight to grow in, and gather them there: for betony that grows in the shade is far better than that which grows in the sun, because it delights in the shade; so also such herbs as delight to grow near water, should be gathered near it, though haply you may find some of them upon dry ground.

3. The leaves of such herbs, as run up to seed, are not so good when they are in flower as before, (some few excepted, the leaves of which are seldom or never used) in such cases, if through negligence forgotten, you had better take the top and the flowers than the leaf.

Culpeper's Complete Herbal (Directions)

PARSLEY

An Ancient Aid to Youth and Beauty

Properties

Relaxant • Diuretic • Antiseptic • Tonic • Depurative • Uterine tonic • Digestive
Antirheumatic

Folk remedies from the past
Probably the most widely used culinary herb, parsley has been accredited with various magical powers since the times of ancient Greece and Rome. Dedicated to Persephone, Queen of Hades, it was eaten at funeral banquets and placed on tombstones to bring good luck to the departed.

• Romans tucked parsley inside their togas to provide protection and gladiators ate it to increase their strength.

• In early European traditions parsley root was used to treat jaundice, malaria, and dropsy.

• Parsley seed was once a remedy for the plague.

Parsley is rich in vitamin C, pro-vitamin A, iron, calcium, potassium, phosphorus, manganese, sulphur, copper, and silicon. Its volatile oils, notably apiol, have antiseptic properties that help to combat infections and reduce fevers.

Internal

Raw parsley is useful in the treatment of iron-deficiency anaemia as its vitamin C content enhances iron absorption. It stimulates the appetite by increasing stomach activity and secretions, and enhances digestion and absorption, making it an excellent tonic particularly during convalescence. Its relaxing effect in the digestive tract relieves flatulence, colic, and indigestion. As a diuretic, it relieves fluid retention and speeds the elimination of toxins from the system, making it an excellent remedy for arthritis and gout. A decoction of the seeds relaxes the smooth muscle throughout the body and relieves headaches, migraines, asthma, abdominal cramps, irritable bladder, and indigestion. It stimulates the circulation and benefits the nervous system, reducing lethargy and anxiety. Although parsley can be beneficial after childbirth to ensure normal readjustment of the uterus and to increase the flow of breast milk, it has a stimulating effect on the muscles of the uterus and so all parts of the plant should be avoided during pregnancy.

Chewing fresh parsley leaves removes the odour of onions and garlic from the breath.

External

Crushed, fresh leaves applied to the breasts during lactation relieve engorgement and help prevent abscesses. They also relieve irritation from insect stings and make an antiseptic dressing for cuts and wounds. Fresh parsley juice can be used locally for toothache, to combat head lice, and to give lustre to the hair.

CAUTION
Do not use during pregnancy.

PLANTAIN

Healer of Wounds, Antidote to Poisons

Properties

Astringent • Anti-inflammatory • Expectorant • Antiseptic • Laxative

Plantain's folk use as an antidote to poisons may derive from its ability to clear heat and eliminate toxins from the body; it is used to great effect in the treatment of fevers, infections, and inflammation, as well as to clear boils and abscesses, septicaemia, and many skin conditions.

Internal

Plantain is one of the best remedies for catarrh. It reduces the secretion of mucus, making it extremely useful for colds, sinusitis, bronchial congestion, glue ear, earache, hay fever, and asthma. Its expectorant action helps liquefy phlegm and aids its expulsion from the chest, while its antiseptic action helps to combat infection. It is also used as a soothing remedy for stomach and bowel infections, and urinary problems such as cystitis, prostatitis, and urethritis. Its zinc content influences prostate gland function, making it a useful medicine for prostatic enlargement. The mucilage in plantain has a soothing effect throughout the body, protecting mucous linings, relaxing spasm, and relieving irritation. The astringent tannins reduce bleeding and inflammation, which explains plantain's traditional use for diarrhoea, vomiting of blood, and excessive menstruation. Plantain's seeds make an excellent bulk laxative. The seed coat swells in water to form a soothing gel, ideal for chronic constipation and irritable bowel syndrome.

External

Plantain's action as a wound healer is due to its silica and zinc content, which stems bleeding and speeds repair. Apply crushed fresh leaves to nettle stings and insect bites and stings, cuts, burns, sprains, bruises, ulcers, and haemorrhoids. An infusion of plantain makes a good eyewash for inflamed eyes and eyelids.

Folk remedies from the past

Famed for its healing powers, the Greeks and Romans used plantain for sores and skin infections, as well as the bite of a mad dog.

• Plantain tends to grow along paths, which was of great comfort to pilgrims in Saxon times, who used it for sprains and minor injuries incurred along the way.

• The North American Indians had two names for plantain: "white man's foot", as it grew where white men had settled, and "snakeweed", due to its use as an antidote to venomous bites. The name *Plantago* comes from *planta*, meaning the sole of the foot, referring to the broad-leafed plantain's shape.

In India, the seeds of Plantago psyllium are used as a diuretic for urinary problems, for diarrhoea, and as a remedy for worms. Put 1–2 teaspoons in half a glass of water and leave to swell for 30 minutes. Take last thing at night.

CHAMOMILE

A Calming Digestive with Excellent Healing Properties

Properties

Relaxant • Antiseptic • Anti-inflammatory • Antihistamine • Digestive • Analgesic

The main constituent of chamomile is a beautiful blue volatile oil containing azulenes, which give it such a distinctive fragrance. It is a wonderful relaxant, particularly to the nervous system and the digestion, and is an excellent remedy for insomnia, nightmares, and calming fractious children. Women have taken chamomile for years as a remedy for pregnancy sickness and as a relaxant during childbirth. It also relieves mastitis, painful periods, and premenstrual tension.

Internal

Chamomile relaxes smooth muscle throughout the body. In the digestive tract it relieves tension and spasm, and is useful for colic, abdominal pain, wind, distension, and stress-related digestive problems. By regulating peristalsis it treats both diarrhoea and constipation, and soothes all kinds of digestive upsets. The bitters stimulate the flow of bile and the digestive juices, enhancing appetite and improving digestion. Chamazulene in the volatile oil acts as an anti-inflammatory, while bisabolol speeds healing, both of which are beneficial for gastritis and peptic ulcers. It makes a wonderful antiseptic remedy for bacterial and fungal infections, as well as fevers, colds, and flu.

External

Chamomile is a great healer. Its antiseptic oils exert a soothing and anti-inflammatory effect on the skin, and stimulate repair. Apply the dilute oil, or compresses of chamomile tea, to ulcers, sores, and burns. Chamomile is also a natural antihistamine, and its anti-allergic effects can be put to good use by inhaling it with steam for asthma, hay fever, catarrh, and sinusitis. The tea makes a good antiseptic mouthwash and gargle, and can be used for sore nipples and as a vaginal douche.

Folk remedies from the past

The Egyptians revered chamomile for its medicinal virtues, particularly its power to cure "ague" and fevers, and dedicated it to the sun.

• Chamomile was one of the nine sacred herbs of the Saxons, who used it widely as a sedative and calming medicine for the stomach. In the Middle Ages, it was strewn around the insanitary halls of castles and great houses to keep foul smells and infection at bay.

• The Greeks and Romans considered chamomile one of the best remedies for menstrual disorders. Its Latin name; *Matricaria chamomilla*; comes from the word matrix, meaning mother or womb.

• Chamomile is a great pain reliever. It can be taken for headaches and migraines, toothache, and neuralgia. Massaged into painful inflamed joints, dilute chamomile oil will bring relief to sufferers of sciatica.

Sit in a bowl of chamomile tea to soothe cystitis and haemorrhoids.

Chamomile is a well-established favourite among garden herbs. There are two kinds of chamomile used medicinally: German chamomile and Roman chamomile. Their properties are almost identical, but German chamomile may be preferable as it is less bitter. Roman chamomile is well known for planting in lawns, paths, and arbours, where it releases a pleasing fragrance as it is trodden on. In 1629, Parkinson wrote: "it is a common hearbe, well knowne and is planted of the rootes in alleyes and walkes and on bankes to sit on ... the use thereof is very much both to warm and to comfort and to ease paines".

DANDELION

A Much Maligned Weed With Remarkable Medicinal Properties

Properties

Cholagogue • Detoxifying • Diuretic • Laxative • Antirheumatic

Folk remedies from the past

Said to originate from central Asia, the dandelion has long been respected throughout the world as a valuable medicine .

- As the traditional name "piss-a-bed" suggests, dandelion has been used as a diuretic remedy for water retention, cellulite, urinary infections, and prostate problems.
- A decoction of dandelion roots and leaves is a folk remedy for dissolving urinary stones and gravel.

Roasted and ground dandelion roots make a caffeine-free substitute for coffee.

Add young dandelion leaves to salads to make an excellent tonic in the spring.

CAUTION

Take care not to give dandelion juice to children as it can cause nausea, vomiting, and diarrhoea.

The dandelion is highly nutritious and the whole of the plant can be used as a medicine. The leaves are delicious in salads or cooked as spinach. They are rich in minerals, especially potassium and iron, and in vitamins B, C, and pro-vitamin A; the roots contain sterols, insulin, sugars, pectin, and glycosides.

Internal

Dandelion is best known as a gently detoxifying bitter tonic that cleanses the system by increasing the elimination of toxins, wastes, and pollutants through the liver and kidneys. The bitter taste of both root and leaf stimulates the bitter receptors in the mouth which, by reflex, activate the whole of the digestive tract and the liver. By increasing the flow of digestive juices, dandelion enhances the appetite and eases digestion; by increasing the flow of bile it cleanses the liver – the major detoxifying organ of the body. Dandelion root is beneficial in liver problems, jaundice, hepatitis, gall-bladder infections and gall stones; also for complaints such as tiredness, irritability, headaches, and skin problems associated with a sluggish liver, It is beneficial in diabetes and hypoglycaemia (low blood sugar) due to its stimulating effect on the pancreas, where it increases the secretion of insulin. The root is slightly laxative. Since the leaves have a diuretic action, improving elimination of uric acid from the body, they are helpful in the treatment of gout, arthritis, and rheumatism. Normally, diuretics leach potassium from the body, but dandelion's high potassium content replaces any that is lost.

External

As a cure for warts, apply the white juice of the dandelion over a few weeks. An infusion of the leaves and flowers makes a good wash for ulcers and skin complaints.

BURDOCK

A Bitter Tonic for Cleansing the System

Properties

Depurative • Antibiotic • Diuretic • Laxative • Hypoglycaemic • Digestive
Anti-inflammatory

Burdock is a large, attractive-looking member of the thistle family, found in fields and on roadsides all over the world. Despite its bitter taste, some people treat it as a vegetable – the Japanese eat the roots boiled in salt water.

Internal

Together, the roots, leaves, and seeds of burdock have an action in almost every part of the body, contributing to its overall cleansing effect. The whole plant is bitter, stimulating digestion and liver function, and activating the pancreas. It strengthens a weak digestion, relieves indigestion, and is a mild laxative. The mucilaginous fibres absorb chemical residues, metabolic wastes, and metal contaminants in the gut, bind them and carry them through the bowel to be eliminated. Burdock's antibacterial and antifungal properties help to combat infection, such as candidiasis, and make it excellent for re-establishing a normal bacterial population in the gut after antibiotics. It is also useful for treating skin disease as it improves the action of the sebaceous glands. Burdock is an effective treatment for chronic inflammatory diseases such as gout, rheumatism, and arthritis. It is best taken in small amounts at the beginning of treatment, particularly when the symptoms are severe, to avoid aggravation. The whole plant has diuretic properties aiding the elimination of toxins.

External

A burdock poultice can be used on poorly healing wounds to speed repair, and on ulcers, bruises, sores, and inflammatory skin conditions such as acne, boils and eczema. For impetigo, cold sores, ringworm, athlete's foot, and candidiasis, try bathing the skin with a decoction of burdock, or massaging it into your scalp as a hair tonic.

Folk remedies from the past

Since the Middle Ages burdock has been a popular medicine, especially since it is reputed to have cured Henry VIII of syphilis. It was also a remedy for leprosy.

- Culpeper recommended burdock for bites of serpents and mad dogs, due to its efficient cleansing and detoxifying properties. He also wrote that "the seed is much commended to break the stone", referring to its effect on urinary stones.
- North American Indians used burdock to strengthen the womb before and after childbirth, and to lend stamina in labour.
- Burdock has been used traditionally to lower blood sugar in diabetes. Modern research has confirmed that the bitter glycosides have a reflex action on the pancreas, and the root is rich in inulin, a starch which does not stress the pancreas.

A hot decoction of burdock causes sweating and clears toxins from tissues via the skin. This reduces a fever and speeds recovery from eruptive infections such as measles.

ROSEMARY

Prince of Aromatic Herbs

Properties

Antiseptic • Antibacterial • Antifungal • Relaxant • Anti-ageing
Astringent • Memory enhancer • Diuretic

Native to the Mediterranean from where it derives its name, *Rosmarinus* – dew of the sea, rosemary has long been considered a wonderful tonic, particularly to the heart, brain, and nervous system. The Renaissance herbalist Wilhelm Ryff said of rosemary: "The spirits of the Heart and entire body feel joy from this drink, which dispels all despondency and worry".

Internal

By increasing blood flow to the head, rosemary stimulates the brain and heightens concentration, which may account for its reputation for improving memory. Its ability to relax tense muscles in this area also makes it an excellent remedy for headaches and migraine. Rosemary has a warming effect, stimulating the heart and circulation, dispelling cold and winter blues, improving circulation and vitality, and aiding digestion. It helps to clear toxins from the body by enhancing liver function and by increasing the flow of urine, and is useful for arthritis and gout. Like other aromatic herbs, rosemary contains antiseptic volatile oils which enhance the immune system. A hot tea helps bring down fevers, clear phlegm, and chase away coughs, colds, sore throats, and chest infections, and by relieving bronchial spasm it can be helpful in asthma.

External

A bath with a few drops of rosemary oil is an excellent pick-me-up when you feel tired and achy. Rub the dilute oil on inflamed joints, on to your scalp to check hair fall, or on to the skin for infections such as scabies or lice. Rubbed into the temples it soothes headaches and dispels lethargy. Use the tea as a vaginal douche for infections, and as a mouthwash for bleeding gums.

Folk remedies from the past

Thought to bring luck and joy, rosemary used to be woven into royal crowns and bridal veils. Anne of Cleves, the fourth bride of Henry VIII, is said to have worn a circlet of gold and precious gems intertwined with rosemary – not that it brought her much luck!

- In Italy and Portugal, rosemary was a symbol of fidelity, which is why it was placed in the slippers of the bride and groom, to ensure loyalty.
- Rosemary was believed to protect from pestilence and disease as well as evil and witchcraft. Tubfuls of dried rosemary leaves were burnt to fumigate the atmosphere and dispel disease in hospitals and homes of the sick.
- Rosemary was a key ingredient of Hungary water, a remedy given in the 14th century to Queen Izabella of Hungary. Aged 72 and afflicted with gout, after a year of using it she had recovered her health and beauty so much that the King of Poland proposed to her. Recent research has shown that it is a powerful antioxidant with an ability to slow the ageing process.

CAUTION Do not use during pregnancy.

Rosemary has been used as a folk remedy for a whole host of ailments: fainting, nervousness, anxiety, exhaustion, lethargy, depression, insomnia, apoplexy, dim sight, dizziness, drowsiness, feebleness, foolishness, palsy, convulsions, even insanity! It was worn in a linen cloth tied around the right arm to make the wearer 'light and merrie". It used to be sold in apothecaries as a cure for hangovers, and was considered to be an excellent cleanser of the system. The tannins in the leaves are astringent, and help to check bleeding and reduce excessive menstruation. Its relaxant effect also relieves period pains.

SAGE

An Ancient Elixir of Life

Properties

Antiseptic • Digestive • Astringent • Tonic • Antioxidant • Oestrogenic

Folk remedies from the past

The ancient Greeks called sage the "immortality herb", so great are its curative properties. Similarly, the ancient Egyptians praised it as a life saver. No wonder the origin of sage's botanical name, *Salvia*, means "to save".

• Throughout the Middle Ages, prescriptions for elixirs of life featured sage for its rejuvenating action.

• Sage was traditionally used in cooking rich and heavy foods as an aid to digestion.

• The ancient Romans used sage as a remedy for infertility. A couple had to remain apart for four days and regularly drink sage tea. Once reunited they apparently enjoyed a second honeymoon – said to have unfailing results!

CAUTION

Do not take large amounts of sage over long time periods. Avoid using sage during pregnancy and breast-feeding.

One of the most valued herbs of antiquity, sage is highly antiseptic and has been revered since the time of the ancient Egyptians as a rejuvenating tonic and for its ability to fight off infection – even the plague.

Internal

Taken at the first symptom of any respiratory infection, sage makes an excellent remedy for tonsillitis, bronchitis, asthma, catarrh, and sinusitis. Sage's astringent and expectorant properties also help to expel phlegm from the chest and reduce catarrh. Drinks and inhalations of the tea will enhance the immune system and speed infections on their way. Sage's volatile oils relax the muscles of the digestive tract, while the bitters stimulate digestion by encouraging the flow of digestive juices and bile. You can take sage to improve appetite, settle the stomach, and relieve colic, indigestion, nausea, diarrhoea, colitis, and liver complaints. Sage's diuretic action makes it a useful cleanser in toxic conditions and for arthritis and gout. Sage is recommended for regulating menstruation and for period cramps. Its astringent properties help reduce heavy bleeding, while its oestrogenic effect makes it an excellent remedy for menopausal problems, particularly hot flushes.

External

Sage is a first-rate antiseptic and astringent for cuts and wounds and it speeds tissue repair. You can apply sage tea to burns, sores, ulcers, insect bites, and skin problems; use in a liniment or compress for strains, arthritis, and neuralgia. You can use sage tea as a gargle for sore throats, as a mouthwash for mouth ulcers and inflamed gums, and as a douche to relieve vaginal irritation and infections such as candidiasis.

COMFREY

An Excellent Healing Remedy for Wounds and Broken Bones

Properties

Nutritious • Demulcent • Astringent • Restorative • Healing

Comfrey is an old favourite in cottage and physic gardens. Not only are its leaves highly nutritious, but for thousands of years it has been employed to promote the repair of wounds, ulcers, and fractured or broken bones. Its leaves and roots contain mucilage and tannins, as well as allantoin – a remarkable substance that stimulates the production of connective tissue responsible for forming cartilage and bone.

Internal

Comfrey leaves can be taken to heal any tissues they can reach, particularly in the respiratory, digestive, and urinary systems. The astringent effect of the tannins reduces bleeding, draws tissues together, and inhibits infection; the mucilage soothes, cools, and moistens where there is heat and inflammation. So comfrey is an ideal remedy for sore throats and laryngitis, and a soothing expectorant for dry coughs and bronchitis. In the gut, comfrey soothes irritation and helps to heal gastritis and gastric or duodenal ulcers. In the urinary system, it relaxes spasm, soothes cystitis, and clears irritation. Comfrey can also help relieve painful and inflamed conditions such as gout, arthritis, sprains, tendonitis, and fractured bones.

External

Comfrey is a prime first-aid remedy when applied to the skin. The allantoin diffuses into the underlying tissues, where it can accelerate healing and closure of a fractured bone. The mucilaginous content of fresh roots and leaves seeps into the injured skin of wounds, sores, and ulcers; as it dries and contracts, it draws the sides of the wound together, and seals it against infection. A poultice or ointment can be used for bruises, strains, arthritis and gout, varicose veins, and burns. A hot poultice draws pus from boils and splinters from the skin.

Folk remedies from the past

For thousands of years, comfrey's wonderful healing abilities have been celebrated. Rural names such as knitbone, bruisewort, and boneset indicate its reputation.

- Comfrey baths were popular before the wedding night to attempt to repair the hymen and thereby apparently restore virginity!
- Comfrey has an ancient reputation as a nourishing restorative herb, useful in depleted conditions, anaemia, and convalescence.
- In Ireland comfrey was eaten to cure poor circulation and "impoverished blood".

A decoction of the root or an infusion of the leaves makes a good eyewash for inflamed eyes, a gargle for sore throats, and a mouthwash for bleeding gums.

ROSE

A Symbol of Love and Beauty

Properties

Cooling • Detoxifying • Tonic • Decongestant • Astringent • Antidepressant • Immune enhancer • Laxative • Diuretic

Folk remedies from the past

The Greeks used the champagne rose as a tonic, while Pliny listed 32 remedies made by the Romans from roses, including the dog rose which was thought to cure the bites of mad dogs.

- Roses were associated with merriment and wine – they were scattered on feast days and worn as garlands to prevent drunkenness. Roman women sprinkled themselves with dried rose petals after bathing, brightened their eyelids with rose oil, and sucked rose pastilles to sweeten their breath.
- Avicenna, a 10th-century Arab doctor, was the first to make rose water. He used rose jelly to cure spitting of blood.
- Early North American settlers drank rose tea as a cure for heartburn, and a decoction of rose hips to ease the stomach.

CAUTION

Avoid roses during pregnancy as they can stimulate the uterus.

The perfumed rose is considered the most beautiful flower in the world. Many a poet has sung praises of its beauty and the enchanting nature of its scent, although it has other virtues, too, notably as a medicine.

Internal

Both the leaves and petals of roses have a cooling effect and when taken in tea can bring down fevers and clear toxins from the body. They also enhance immunity and strengthen the lungs, making it an excellent tonic for people with low resistance. Rose petal tea will relieve cold and flu symptoms, catarrh, and bronchial congestion. Roses combat infection in the digestive tract and help re-establish a normal bacterial population after antibiotics. The petals act as a decongestant in the female reproductive system, relieving pain and heavy periods, and enhancing fertility and sexual desire. In men, they are used to treat impotence. Their diuretic action hastens the elimination of wastes through the urinary system. The astringent tannins staunch bleeding, dry phlegm, and arrest discharges and diarrhoea. They also make an effective liver remedy. Rose hips and petals have an uplifting and calming effect on the nervous system, lifting depression and dispelling fatigue, while the oil is recommended for emotional problems related to love (or lack of it) and sexuality.

External

Rose water cleanses and tones the skin, smoothes out wrinkles, and clears blemishes, acne, and spots. It soothes sore eyes, aids tissue repair, and reduces the swelling of bruises and sprains. An infusion of rose petals makes an effective mouthwash and gargle, and a douche for vaginal discharge. Treat dry chapped lips with rose oil or ointment.

Just before World War II, the hips of the wild rose were found to contain one of the most abundant sources of vitamin C in the plant kingdom. They are also rich in vitamins A, B, and K. They were made into rose hip syrup (which was then rationed during the war) to ensure children's resistance to infection and to treat the common cold. This syrup or decoction made from the empty seed cases makes a useful remedy for diarrhoea, stomach and menstrual cramps, nausea, and indigestion. You can use it as a laxative, for kidney problems, and as a depurative. Its delicate aromatic taste makes it useful in medicines to mask the taste of other herbs.

NETTLE

A Nutritious Spring Tonic

Properties

Antihaemorrhagic • Diuretic • Astringent • Restorative
Galactagogue • Detoxifying

Folk remedies from the past

Once used to make beer, paper, and even army uniforms, the fibrous nettle leaf has been put to more uses than almost any other herb.

• A tincture of the seeds is a traditional remedy for fevers and lung disorders, and a decoction of the roots was a well-known remedy for pleurisy.

• "Urtication" (stinging of the body with nettles to stimulate the circulation) is a very old Russian tradition. It was used for coughs, paralysis, muscle wasting, sciatica, and rheumatism, and to stimulate menstruation.

• In World War II, nettles were gathered for their high chlorophyll content and used to dress infected wounds and speed their healing.

For a springtime tonic, add nettle tops to soups and stews. Cook them like spinach or make them into a tea. Hang up a bunch of fresh nettles in the kitchen to keep flies away from food.

Apply fresh juice to insect bites and stings as well as the sting of a nettle.

Nettles are highly nutritious, rich in vitamins A and C and in minerals, particularly potassium, iron, and silica, and so make a nourishing tonic for anaemia, weakness, and debility, and during convalescence. By stimulating the liver and kidneys, nettles help to cleanse the body of toxins and wastes, and can be used in all kinds of skin disease.

Internal

The nettle's diuretic action helps cleanse the kidneys and relieve fluid retention, cystitis, urethritis, stones, and gravel. By increasing the excretion of uric acid, nettles relieve gout and other arthritic conditions. They act as a stimulating tonic to the digestive tract, and are beneficial in diarrhoea, flatulence, ulcers, and worms. They have also been shown to reduce blood sugar levels. All parts of the nettle have been used for respiratory problems. Their cleansing and astringent properties help clear catarrhal congestion and relieve allergies, such as hay fever and asthma. For women, the nettle is an excellent astringent remedy for heavy bleeding and menstrual irregularities, to increase milk in nursing mothers, and as a restorative during the menopause.

External

The stinging hairs of the fresh nettle contain formic acid and histamine, both of which help relieve arthritis. The sting, by increasing the flow of blood to the skin and inducing inflammation over an already inflamed joint, removes fluids and toxins from the area and thus relieves the pain and swelling. As an astringent fresh nettles or tincture will stop bleeding of cuts and wounds and nose bleeds and speed healing of burns and scalds. An infusion makes an excellent mouthwash and gargle and a stimulating hair tonic.

DOCK

A Wonderful Detoxifying Remedy to Invigorate the System and Clear the Skin

Properties

Tonic • Laxative • Astringent • Cholagogue • Liver remedy • Diuretic

Yellow curled dock is native to both Europe and Asia, and is widespread in North and South America. The ability of its long, yellow taproot to extract iron from the soil makes it an excellent remedy for anaemia.

Internal

Anthraquinones in the root have a gentle laxative effect, while astringent tannins reduce excess activity in the gut and soothe irritation in the gut lining, making dock a gentle cleanser for long-term treatment of constipation. It can also be used for bowel infections and peptic ulcers. Bitter glycosides in the root stimulate the liver and enhance bile production, improving a sluggish liver, weak digestion, distension, and wind. Its diuretic properties increase urine production and the elimination of toxins, explaining its old use for gout, cystitis, water retention, and urinary gravel and stones. Dock's ability to mobilize congested blood and lymph, and to eliminate toxins from the tissues, makes it an excellent detoxifying addition to remedies for skin disease, arthritis, rheumatism, and chronic lymphatic congestion. It is also effective in the treatment of menstrual irregularities and uterine fibroids. Its high iron content and tonic effect on the liver explain its use as a revitalizing remedy for general debility, mental lethargy, convalescence, headaches, low spirits, and irritability.

External

Dock's cooling and healing properties are well known for the treatment of all inflammatory skin conditions. It can be used as a mouthwash to treat gum infections and mouth ulcers, as a gargle for laryngitis and sore throats, as an eyewash for dry, inflamed eyes, and as a lotion for cuts and wounds, sores and ulcers, and infections on the skin.

Folk remedies from the past

Dock has long been used since the time of the ancient Greeks, who recognized its value as a cleanser of toxins from the system and to treat digestive problems.

•. In 1633, Gerard recommended powdered dock root in wine as an astringent to stop the "bloudie flixe" and said that the boiled roots made into an ointment "helpeth the itche".

• Dock seeds were a traditional remedy for dysentery, diarrhoea, and haemorrhages, and for coughs and bleeding from the lungs.

• American Indians applied pulverized dock root to cuts and crushed leaves to boils.

• Dock's most famous action is underscored by the old saying: "Nettle out, dock in. Dock removes the nettle sting."

Take a decoction or tincture of dock root regularly to treat skin ailments such as weeping eczema, psoriasis, nettle rash, and boils.

CAUTION

Do not use during pregnancy.

MARIGOLD

A Magic Plant to Comfort the Heart and Heal the Body

Properties

Stimulant • Antiseptic • Astringent • Diuretic • Anti-inflammatory • Depurative
Oestrogenic

Folk remedies from the past

The Romans used marigold tea to relieve fevers, and the juice of the crushed flower as a treatment for warts.

• In the Middle Ages, St Hildegarde and Albert the Great used marigold for intestinal troubles, liver obstructions, and insect and snake bites.

• Marigold's Latin name, *Calendula*, comes from *calends*, meaning the first day of every month, because in its native Mediterranean climate it comes into flower on the first day of every month of the year.

• Renowned as an antiseptic and anti-inflammatory styptic, it was used for battle wounds during the American Civil War and World War I. The famous gardener Gertrude Jekyll sent crates of marigolds from her Sussex estate to be used in field hospitals in France.

CAUTION

Do not use during pregnancy.

The charming marigold with its cheerful orange flower that opens as the sun rises and closes as it sets, is a familiar sight in cottage gardens. Its medicinal properties have been well known to herbalists throughout history.

Internal

A hot infusion of marigold stimulates the circulation and causes sweating, thereby clearing the body of toxins and bringing out eruptions such as measles and chicken pox. It strengthens the immune system, reduces lymphatic congestion, and is an excellent remedy for colds and coughs, viruses such as flu and herpes, and fungal infections including candida. It has been used to treat pelvic and bowel infections, including enteritis and dysentery. The astringent and antiseptic properties, provided by volatile oils, tannins, and a yellow resin called calendulin, exert a beneficial influence in the digestive system. Marigold can be used for gastritis, peptic ulcers, soothing inflammation, drying catarrh, checking diarrhoea, and stopping bleeding. The bitters stimulate the liver and gall bladder, increasing the secretion of enzymes and bile, and helping to cleanse the body of toxins. Marigold also acts as a diuretic, providing another exit route (via urine) for toxins, and has been used as a cleansing remedy for arthritis and gout.

External

Marigold is best known as an antiseptic healer and first-aid remedy. Used in tincture, as an infusion, or simply by crushing the flower, its astringent action staunches bleeding, promotes healing, and resolves infection, inflammation, and swelling. It can heal chilblains, piles, varicose veins, ulcers, eczema, acne, cradle cap, cold sores, burns, sunburn, insect bites and stings, warts, corns, and calluses.

The name marigold refers to its traditional use in church festivals in the Middle Ages, being one of the flowers dedicated to the Virgin Mary. That it should be named after a female saint may be due to its value to women, for it has a particular affinity for the female reproductive system. It is used to treat tumours and cysts, such as fibroids and ovarian cysts, as well as cysts and congestion in the breast. It also regulates periods, reduces tension in the uterine muscles, and relieves menstrual cramps and heavy bleeding. It acts like oestrogen, helping to relieve menopausal symptoms, such as hot flushes. Marigold also aids contractions during childbirth.

YARROW

Famous Healing Herb Used by Achilles, the Greek Warrior

Properties

Anti-inflammatory • Antiseptic • Astringent • Detoxifying
Diuretic • Antidepressant

Folk remedies from the past

Yarrow is a very versatile medicinal plant, whose virtues have been praised since the time of the ancient Greeks. It is named after the Greek warrior Achilles who used it to staunch the bleeding of his companions' wounds. In Greek mythology, Achilles' warlike prowess and invulnerability were due to rubbing his body with yarrow; the omission of his right heel was said to have led to his downfall.

• Yarrow has a reputation in folklore as a nerve tonic. In Germany, it was used for melancholy and moodiness, and in old England it was added to wedding bouquets to guarantee seven years of happiness. It has been used for tension, anxiety, nervous palpitations, debility, and as a tonic after illness to lift the spirits.

• In World War I, soldiers carried yarrow for use as a first-aid dressing.

The dark green aromatic leaves of yarrow are feathery, finely divided, and very numerous, hence its Latin name *millefolium*, meaning a thousand leaves. Yarrow has many constituents which contribute to its healing powers. The volatile oils are anti-inflammatory and antiseptic, the tannins and resins are astringent, while the silica promotes tissue repair.

Internal

Yarrow is an excellent remedy for regulating the whole of the digestive system. It stimulates appetite, enhances digestion and absorption, and relaxes tension and spasm. Its astringent properties curb diarrhoea and stem any tendency to bleeding. Its antiseptic and anti-inflammatory properties treat infections and inflammatory conditions, such as gastritis and enteritis, and the bitters improve liver and gall bladder function. Yarrow is ideal for infections, catarrh, and fevers, especially in children, and is best taken in hot infusion at the start of sore throats, colds, and flu. By stimulating the circulation it causes sweating and thereby helps to clear toxins from the system. It is an excellent remedy for eruptive diseases such as measles and chicken pox as it helps to bring out the rash. It reduces blood pressure and relieves stasis of the blood, as in varicose veins, and constriction of the blood vessels, as in Raynaud's disease. Its diuretic properties aid detoxification, making it useful for fluid retention, cystitis, irritable bladder, stones, and gravel.

External

Yarrow is used to treat cuts, wounds, burns, ulcers, bruises, whitlows, haemorrhoids, varicose veins, and eczema. You can use an infusion as a douche for vaginal discharges, as an eyebath for sore inflamed eyes, as a cleanser and toner for the skin, and as a rinse for falling hair and dandruff.

Try chewing fresh yarrow leaves to ease toothache.

CAUTION

Avoid taking yarrow in pregnancy.

THYME

A Stimulating and Warming Herb

Properties

Antiseptic • Expectorant • Diuretic • Sedative • Astringent
Carminative • Antioxidant

Both common thyme and wild thyme are powerful antiseptics, enhancing the immune system's fight against bacterial, viral, and fungal infections. The main component of thyme's volatile oil, thymol, is used in antiseptic creams, lotions, mouthwashes, and toothpastes.

Internal

Thyme has a wonderfully pungent taste and warming properties, helping to stimulate the circulation and dispelling cold in winter. Thyme is excellent for coughs related either to nerves or infections such as bronchitis, pneumonia, and pleurisy, and it is especially suitable for children. By relaxing the bronchial tubes, it helps relieve asthma and whooping cough, while its expectorant action shifts phlegm. In the digestive system, its relaxing effects soothe wind, colic, irritable bowel syndrome, and spastic colon. Its astringent tannins protect the gut from irritation and reduce diarrhoea while its antiseptic oils fight infections such as dysentery and gastroenteritis. It is particularly beneficial to those suffering from candidiasis or who are taking antibiotics, as it helps to re-establish the normal bacterial population in the bowel. For the nervous system, it makes a good remedy for exhaustion, anxiety, insomnia, and depression. As a diuretic, it helps relieve water retention, urinary tract infections, rheumatism, and gout. Research suggests that its volatile oils act as an antioxidant.

External

Thyme oil can be used in warming liniments and lotions for arthritis, muscular pain, and itching, and as a disinfectant. An infusion or the tincture make an effective antiseptic mouthwash and gargle, and a douche for thrush. It is also an excellent inhalant for colds, coughs, catarrh, asthma, and sinusitis.

Folk remedies from the past

Thyme's name comes from the Greek *thyein* meaning "to smoke", as the ancient Greeks made it into incense. The ancient Egyptians and Etruscans used thyme in preparations to embalm their dead. The Romans slept on beds of thyme, inhaling its sweet aroma to cure melancholy.

- Thyme was used as a strewing herb to protect against epidemics of leprosy and the plague.
- Traditionally, thyme was used as a remedy for vertigo and migraine. Tincture of thyme taken half an hour before breakfast was said to cure worms.

A strong infusion of thyme in your bath will help stimulate your circulation and throw off chills and lethargy.

CAUTION

Do not use during pregnancy.

LAVENDER

An Exquisitely Scented Nerve Tonic to Balance the Emotions

Properties

Relaxant • Antidepressant • Restorative • Antiseptic • Decongestant • Expectorant
Detoxifying • Diuretic

Folk remedies from the past
In the New Testament, St Mark refers to spikenard (lavender) as an oil of great value. The woman who came to Christ with an alabaster box of spikenard ointment "brake the box and poured it on his head".

• The Romans used lavender to perfume their baths, hence its name which comes from *lavare*, meaning to wash.

• The Virgin Mary is reputed to have been especially fond of lavender because it protected clothes from insects and "dirty beasts", and also preserved chastity.

• An old restorative remedy for faintness, giddiness, and debility was to inhale or imbibe spirit of lavender, made by soaking flowers in brandy or gin.

• Even lions and tigers in zoos were said to be powerfully affected by lavender's calming effect, and to become docile under its influence.

Lavender has always been one of the best-loved scented herbs. The Greek physician Dioscorides considered that its fragrance surpassed all other perfumes, but it was not venerated solely for this but also for its cleansing and purifying qualities. In fact, lavender has a wonderful restoring effect on mind and body.

Internal

For anxiety, depression, nervousness, and the physical symptoms caused by this (tension, headaches, palpitations, and insomnia), lavender can have a deeply calming effect. In the digestive tract, its relaxing effects soothe away spasm, relieve distension and wind, nausea and indigestion, and stimulate the appetite. Its powerful antiseptic oils are active against bacteria such as diphtheria, streptococcus, and pneumococcus, and its decongestant and expectorant properties make it an excellent remedy for colds, catarrh, and chest infections. Taken as hot tea, lavender causes sweating and reduces fever. By eliminating toxins through the pores and, because of its mild diuretic action, through the urine, it helps to detoxify the body.

External

In aromatherapy, when lavender oil is inhaled or massaged into the skin it is considered a balancer to the emotions. It lifts the spirits, relieves depression, and balances inner disharmony. It also acts as a stimulant to the nervous system, restoring strength and vitality. Applied as a dilute oil, its cooling and antiseptic properties make it a useful disinfectant for cuts and wounds, sores, ulcers, and inflammatory skin conditions. It soothes the pain of bruises and swollen joints, and is an excellent remedy to repel insects and for bites and stings. It is renowned for the treatment of burns as it stimulates tissue repair and minimizes scar formation.

During the Middle Ages and Renaissance, lavender was strewn on the floors of houses and churches to ward off the plague. Housewives placed it in cupboards and drawers to make clothes smell fragrant and deter moths. The 16th-century herbalists recognized its medicinal virtues and recommended it for improving eyesight, relieving headaches, giddiness, and faintness, and to comfort the heart. The Italian herbalist Mattioli said: "it is much used in maladies and those disorders of the brain due to coldness, such as epilepsy, apoplexy, spasms and paralysis."

LEMON BALM

An Ancient Tonic that Lifts the Spirits and Calms the Mind

Properties

Antidepressant • Relaxant • Restorative • Sedative • Antiseptic • Antibacterial
Antiviral • Antihistamine

Folk remedies from the past

The Arabs were the first to extol the virtues of lemon balm, using it to cure epilepsy, mental illness, apoplexy, lethargy, and melancholia, and including it in their elixirs of life.

• Lemon balm was an important ingredient in medieval cordials, used to strengthen the heart and lift the spirits.

• Called Melissa (meaning honey bee) by the Greeks, bee keepers still rub their hives with balm so that the bees will never leave and others will be encouraged to come.

• In France, the leaves were added to cakes to strengthen women for childbirth, and to bring on the afterbirth.

A favourite of cottage gardens, this lemon-scented herb with its refreshing taste and cooling effect originally came from the eastern Mediterranean. It is relaxing and restoring to the whole system, with the added benefit of being an effective antimicrobial remedy for a wide variety of infections.

Internal

Lemon balm lifts the spirits, calms the mind and allays anxiety, improves memory, and aids concentration, making the tea an excellent drink for students. A strong infusion added to a warm bath at night helps calm excitable children and aids sleep. Lemon balm soothes the digestive system and stress-related digestive problems, such as indigestion, gastritis, and peptic ulcers; it also relieves menstrual cramps and premenstrual tension, and reduces pain and spasm in the urinary system. It makes a good remedy for headaches, migraine, vertigo, and buzzing in the ears, and when combined with lime flowers can help to reduce high blood pressure. During the menopause it can help relieve depression and provide support through emotional difficulties.

External

The antibacterial properties of lemon balm make it useful for surgical dressings, and the astringent tannins help to knit wounds together and seal them from infection. A warm poultice of the leaves helps bring boils to a head, and crushed leaves relieve insect stings. The oil acts as an antihistamine, helpful in treating eczema and inflammatory eye conditions. An infusion of the leaves with honey and cider vinegar makes a pleasant gargle. Lemon balm has an antiviral action, making it an excellent remedy for cold sores and shingles. Apply the dilute oil directly.

A hot infusion causes sweating and reduces fever, making a good antiseptic remedy for childhood infections, colds and flu, coughs, and catarrh. It also has an antiviral and antihistamine action, useful for mumps and allergies such as hay fever and rhinitis.

HAWTHORN

Food for the Heart

Properties

Diuretic • Cardiotonic • Astringent • Hypotensive • Vasodilator

Hawthorn's flowers, berries, and leaves all have medicinal value, particularly for conditions of the heart. In fact, hawthorn is the best remedy to strengthen the heart and balance the circulation.

Internal

Hawthorn's vasodilatory effect improves the blood supply to all parts of the body, making it beneficial in the treatment of high blood pressure, particularly that associated with hardening of the arteries, as it has the ability to soften deposits of atherosclerosis. It can also raise low blood pressure to normal and improve blood flow through the coronary arteries, reducing the risk of angina. Elsewhere in the body, hawthorn improves poor circulation associated with both kidney disease and "ageing" arteries, and confusion and poor memory due to reduced blood supply to the brain. It is the ideal treatment for all heart conditions including arrhythmias, palpitations, breathlessness, degenerative heart disease, and heart failure. The leaves, flowers, and berries have a relaxant effect on the digestive tract and they stimulate the appetite, improve digestion, and relieve distension. They also relax the nervous system, relieving anxiety, and nervous palpitations, calming restlessness, and inducing sleep. The berries are astringent and have long been used for diarrhoea. As a diuretic, hawthorn reduces fluid retention, helps dissolve stones or gravel, and can be used to prevent night sweats during the menopause.

External

A decoction of berries makes an astringent gargle and an effective vaginal douche. Combined with the flowers as a lotion, the decoction of berries can be applied to treat skin complaints such as acne rosacea.

Folk remedies from the past

Hawthorn has always been considered a sacred and protecting plant. At Greek wedding feasts guests carried sprigs of hawthorn to symbolize the bride and groom's future happiness and prosperity. In Rome, the nuptial chamber was lit by hawthorn torches.

- Since the Middle Ages hawthorn has been used in folk medicine and recommended for the treatment of heart problems, high blood pressure, pleurisy, gout, insomnia, vertigo, and haemorrhaging.
- A decoction of the bark was used to bring down fevers and a decoction of the berries made an excellent remedy for diarrhoea.
- Sprigs of hawthorn were once attached to babies' cradles to protect them from evil spells.

A decoction of hawthorn flowers and berries can be applied to the face to treat acne.

BORAGE

A Cooling Herb to Bring Courage and Joy

Properties

Cooling • Diuretic • Decongestant • Expectorant • Detoxifying
Astringent • Diaphoretic

Folk remedies from the past
Thought to originate from the Mediterranean countries, borage was brought to Britain by the Romans. In medieval times it was used to promote bravery on the jousting field. In 1597, Gerard noted that a cup of borage flowers "comforteth the heart, purgeth melancholy and quieteth the phrenticke and lunatick person".

• Borage's action on hormones has been recognized for centuries as the leaves and seeds have been used to increase the milk supply of nursing mothers.

Since the ancient Greeks, borage with its beautiful blue star-shaped flower has been a herb to dispel melancholy and bring courage; it is immortalized in a saying known for more than 2000 years: "I Borage, bring always courage."

Internal

This nutritious plant, with its cooling and cleansing properties, makes a useful detoxifying remedy. It has been used as a cordial – a tonic to the heart and to lift the spirits, as well as to calm palpitations, and to restore energy in convalescence. It has a relaxing effect generally and is said to dispel sadness. Modern research has thrown new light on borage's ancient reputation: it stimulates the adrenal glands, the organs of courage, to secrete adrenaline, which is valuable in countering the effects of steroids and when weaning off steroid therapy. The oil pressed from borage seeds makes a good alternative to evening primrose oil for menstrual difficulties, eczema, hay fever, and arthritis. Borage increases sweat production and is a diuretic, speeding the removal of toxins from the body via the skin and urinary system. It also has a decongestant, soothing, and expectorant action in the respiratory system and can be used for catarrh, sore throats, and chest infections, including bronchitis, tracheitis, and pleurisy.

Add a handful of borage flowers and lemon balm leaves to apple or pear juice for a refreshing drink

External

Borage tea makes an effective gargle for sore throats and laryngitis, and a mouthwash for stomatitis and bleeding gums. A poultice of the leaves and flowers can be used for sore skin conditions, such as eczema, and those caused by infection, such as ringworm. Wrapped around inflamed joints, the poultice relieves arthritis and gout.

Bathe itching, inflamed skin as well as sores, ulcers, and wounds in borage tea – the astringent tannins in the leaves help the healing process.

ELDER

The Medicine Chest of the Country People

Properties

Decongestant • Relaxant • Anti-inflammatory • Laxative • Diuretic • Diaphoretic

The whole of the beautiful elder plant has been valued for its practical and medicinal uses for thousands of years. It was such an important remedy that it was treated with great respect by country folk and the dryad that was said to live in the plant was always asked before any part was used.

Internal

A hot infusion of elderflowers taken at the onset of colds, tonsillitis, laryngitis, and flu will help resolve the infection quickly by stimulating the circulation, causing sweating, and cleansing the system of toxins. It can be given to children during eruptive diseases, such as measles and chicken pox, to bring out the rash and speed recovery. The flowers' decongestant action reduces and moves phlegm, relieving colds, catarrh, sinusitis, and bronchial congestion, while its relaxant effect relieves bronchospasm, helpful in asthma. The berries, as well as being used for syrups and wines to treat coughs and colds, make a tasty addition to stewed fruit and act as a laxative. They were also used to treat neuralgia and sciatica. Elderflowers have a diuretic action, relieving fluid retention and eliminating toxins that accumulate in arthritis and gout.

External

Elderflowers have traditionally been used to soothe inflammation and heal ulcers, burns, cuts, and wounds, either using the infusion as a lotion or in an ointment. Distilled elder water makes an excellent facial toner and cleanser. Fresh elder leaves used to be laid on the temples to relieve headaches, or rubbed on the face as an insect deterrent (but beware of reaction in sensitive skins). The root and bark of elder make a useful ointment for eczema and psoriasis, and a decoction can be used as a mouthwash.

Folk remedies from the past

The name elder derives from Ellar or Kindler, because its hollow branches were used to blow through to kindle a fire.

• Until the end of the 19th century elderberry wine was sold on London streets on cold winter days and nights to cheer travellers and workers on their way.

• An elder twig in your pocket was thought to offer protection against rheumatism.

Elderflowers make a delicious cordial. Put 2 kg (4.4lbs) sugar and 2 sliced lemons into a pan with 2 litres (3.5 pints) of water, heat until sugar dissolves, cool, then pour over 25 flower heads. Cover and stand for 2 days, then strain, and dilute 1:3 with water.

CAUTION

The root and bark of the elder are strongly aperient (laxative) and should not be taken unless under medical advice. Avoid them if you are pregnant.

MEADOWSWEET

The Herbal Aspirin

Properties

Analgesic • Astringent • Relaxant • Anti-inflammatory • Diuretic
Antiseptic • Diaphoretic

Folk remedies from the past

In Chaucer's *Knight's Tale*, knights about to enter combat drank Save, a concoction containing meadowsweet. The herb was also used for making beer.

• Meadowsweet was a favourite strewing herb in Tudor times. Gerard said that when strewed, the smell "makes the heart merrie and joyful and delighteth the senses".

• One of the sacred herbs of the Druids, meadowsweet was valued in the past as a remedy for smallpox, dysentery, fevers, diarrhoea, spitting of blood, and piles.

• An old remedy to relieve itching and burning eyes was to apply distilled liquid of meadowsweet flowers.

The medicinal virtues of meadowsweet are very similar to those of aspirin, but without the side effects, which involve irritation and, often, bleeding of the stomach lining. The tannins and mucilage in meadowsweet protect this lining and an anti-inflammatory action actually makes this herb one of the best antacid remedies known.

Internal

Meadowsweet is excellent for any inflammatory condition of the stomach or bowels, for acid indigestion, heartburn, gastritis, peptic ulcers, and hiatus hernia. Its astringent action protects and heals the mucous membranes, making it a good remedy for irritated conditions, including enteritis and diarrhoea. Its mild antiseptic action is helpful where there is infection, and its relaxant properties soothe associated griping and colic. For aches and pains, rheumatism, arthritis, and gout, meadowsweet's anti-inflammatory action provides welcome relief. As a diuretic it helps to eliminate toxic wastes and uric acid which may contribute to inflammatory problems. Meadowsweet's analgesic effect helps to soothe pain, headaches, and neuralgia, and its relaxant properties relieve spasm and induce restful sleep. Its mild antiseptic action makes it good for cystitis and urethritis, fluid retention, and kidney problems.

External

Meadowsweet flowers, which are rich in vitamin C, iron, magnesium, and silica, speed healing of connective tissue and resolve inflammation – they are good for cuts, wounds, ulcers, and skin irritations. Their astringent tannins promote healing and staunch bleeding. Use a decoction of the flowers as a mouthwash for ulcers and bleeding gums.

Make an infusion of the leaves and flowers for colds, flu, and children's infections, such as measles and chicken pox, and to bring down fevers and speed infections on their way.

PEPPERMINT

Pungent and Peppery, Cooling and Warming – All in One Herb!

Properties

Stimulant • Restorative • Analgesic • Anti-inflammatory • Relaxant • Antiseptic
Antibacterial • Antiviral • Antifungal

Peppermint's ability to be both cooling and warming depends on how and where it is used. When taken internally it induces heat and improves the circulation, making it a good general tonic during convalescence. Its refreshing taste, however, is followed by a cooling and numbing effect which is also felt when peppermint is applied externally to the skin.

Internal

Peppermint's long-standing reputation as a heart tonic relieving palpitations, stimulating the heart and circulation, and causing sweating, can also be used to combat chills, fevers, and a whole host of winter ailments. Its relaxing and anti-inflammatory properties make it a wonderful remedy for all conditions associated with pain and spasm, such as stomachache, colic, flatulence, heartburn, indigestion, hiccoughs, headaches, migraine, nausea, and travel sickness. Its tannins help protect the gut from irritation, making peppermint useful for griping in diarrhoea, spastic constipation, ulcerative colitis, and Crohn's disease. Its bitters stimulate the liver and gall bladder, and account for its use in liver cleansing and gall stones.

External

Peppermint oil used to be added to baths as a restorative, rather like smelling salts, and was used as an inhalant during fainting fits and dizziness. Its analgesic properties can be put to good use by applying bruised fresh leaves or lotion to joints swollen by arthritis or gout. The highly antiseptic volatile oils, particularly camphor and menthol, make peppermint a useful disinfectant for cold sores, cuts, and grazes, an inhalant for most infections, or a gargle for sore throats. Peppermint oil can also relieve painful toothache, and is included in ear drops for earache.

Folk remedies from the past

Mints have been used for centuries. The Greeks made perfume from mint's refreshing aroma, as did the Hebrews – the Scribes and Pharisees were rebuked by Jesus for paying too much for it, while neglecting law and justice.

• The Greeks and Romans used mint in crowns for religious ceremonies, and as a cure for digestive ills, headaches, coughs, urinary complaints, insect stings, and snake bites. Roman women were more devious in their use of it: they mixed it with honey to sweeten their breath after drinking wine – a crime which was then punishable by death.

• Ancient Greek soldiers were forbidden peppermint in time of war because of its distracting aphrodisiacal properties.

• Arab men have traditionally drunk mint tea to stimulate their virility, and also as a symbol of friendship and love.

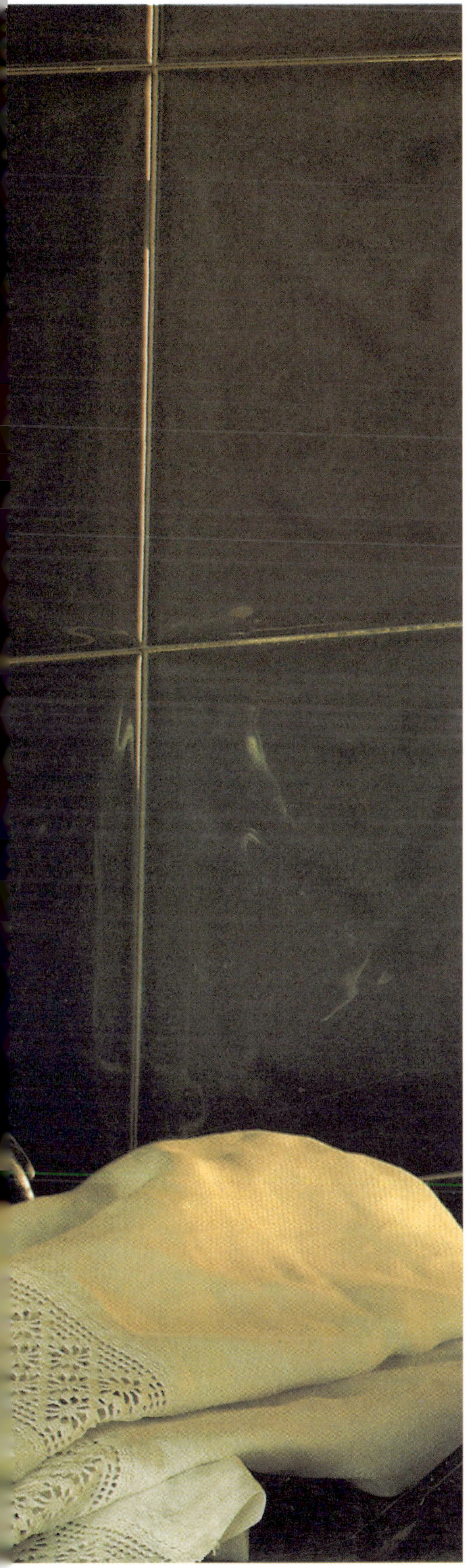

FROM THE

BATHROOM CABINET

Whosoever would keep their mouth, or tongue, or nose, or eyes, or ears, or teeth, from pain or infirmities, let them often use sneezing...for, indeed, most of the infirmities, if not all, which infest those parts, proceed from rheum.

Culpeper's Complete Herbal (Last Legacies 22: A Caution)

If you will keep your teeth from rotting, or aching, wash your mouth continually every morning with juice of lemons, and afterwards rub your teeth either with a sage-leaf, or else with a little nutmeg in powder; also wash your mouth with a little fair water after meats; for the only way to keep teeth sound, and free from pain is to keep them clean.

Culpeper's Complete Herbal (Last Legacies 25: A Caution)

CASTOR OIL

An Ancient Remedy for Clearing the Bowels

Properties

Purgative • Lubricant • Hair conditioner

Folk remedies from the past

Castor oil is one of the most ancient medicines known. Seeds have been found in Egyptian tombs dating back 4000 years. According to the Ebers Papyrus, it was used as a purgative, and for burning in lamps and making ointments.

• Castor oil was a well-known garden plant in the 16th century. It was applied externally to treat skin diseases such as ringworm, and was even used for leprosy.

CAUTION

Keep the seeds away from children, as they contain a very irritant protein called ricin, which can cause violent irritation of the digestive tract. Never use castor oil over a long period, for its initial purgative action is followed by a binding one causing constipation. Nor should it be used following a course of anthelmintics (for worms), as it may cause absorption of these medicines which are only meant to loosen the grip of the parasites.

Castor oil is one of the most useful medicines for evacuating the bowels. It can be used for acute constipation, and to remove irritant or toxic substances from the bowel, arising from, for example, poisoning by food or drugs, or swallowing corrosive substances. Its unpleasant odour and taste make it hard to swallow (unless you hold your nose!), and is best taken with an aromatic such as peppermint oil or lemon juice to disguise the taste.

Internal

Castor oil is so useful because it clears the bowel thoroughly with one dose, and produces a semi-soft stool within 2–8 hours of taking it. It is a bland and soothing oil until it reaches the intestine and is split by the enzyme lipase, whereupon ricinoteic acid, an irritant, is released. This stimulates the whole of the intestines, producing its aperient action. The oil is also lubricating, so that an effortless bowel movement is obtained without any of the violent griping that can be caused by other purgatives. Its gentle action makes it a useful remedy for all ages: the normal dose is 5–15ml for adults and 5ml for children (do not exceed this dosage, as too much may produce nausea, vomiting, and colic).

External

Castor oil is soothing and drawing to the skin. It will soften hard skin on the hands and feet, as well as corns and calluses to ease their removal. When dropped into the eye, castor oil will soothe irritation and soreness caused by the presence of a foreign body. It is also an excellent hair aid, stimulating growth and improving hair condition: a tablespoonful of oil applied before shampooing will revitalize the hair; rubbed into the scalp, it will check dandruff and reduce hair fall.

TINCTURE OF IODINE

A Time-honoured Antiseptic

Properties

Antiseptic • Counter-irritant • Analgesic

For more than a century, iodine has been painted on to the skin to prevent infection entering the body through a cut or abrasion. When applied to unbroken skin it acts powerfully and quickly, and is lethal to bacteria or fungi for several hours. When it comes into contact with blood, however, it is inactivated so should not be applied to wounds until the bleeding has stopped. It can be used for skin infections, parasites such as ringworm and impetigo, and spots, blackheads, and boils. Iodine warms the skin, dilating capillaries that bring blood to relieve pain, accelerate healing, and hasten the removal of toxins. When diluted with water, iodine acts as a mouthwash for inflamed gums and a gargle for sore throats.

Folk remedies from the past

• An old Russian remedy to stop a head cold overnight was to paint the soles of the feet with iodine, put on woollen socks, and sleep in them.

CAUTION:

Iodine can cause blistering. If the tincture is swallowed, take an emetic such as salt or mustard.

FLAX

A Soothing Plant – Wonderful for Dry Skin!

Properties

Demulcent • Anti-inflammatory • Laxative

Flax is one of the oldest-known cultivated plants, whose fibrous stem was and still is made into linen. A tea made from its mucilaginous seeds (linseed) has long been prescribed for soothing a sore throat or hacking cough. The seeds soaked in cold water overnight and mixed with a little licorice act as an excellent bulk laxative, and soothe irritated conditions of the stomach and bowel, such as gastritis, enteritis, and colitis. Linseed oil contains essential fatty acids which are important for the health of the skin, circulation, kidneys, immune system, and the formation of cell membranes and prostaglandins. Apply linseed tea to dry skin or add it to your bath water to soften the skin and ease away tension.

To soothe a troublesome cough and relieve urinary problems, cover 2 tablespoons of linseed and a few slices of lemon with 600ml (1 pint) of boiling water, stir and leave to cool. Strain and sweeten to taste.

Make a poultice by adding boiling water to crushed seeds and stir to a smooth paste. Spread thickly on to a muslin cloth and apply warm to boils, abscesses, and inflammations.

EUCALYPTUS

The Antiseptic Fever Tree

Properties

Antiseptic • Detoxifying • Circulatory stimulant • Decongestant • Diaphoretic

Folk remedies from the past
Indigenous to Australia and Tasmania, eucalyptus was introduced to Europe, Africa, and the Americas in the mid-19th century by German botanist Baron Ferdinand von Muller. He was the first to suggest that the oil may be of use as a disinfectant in fever districts.

• Eucalyptus is a traditional Australian Aboriginal remedy for fevers. Eucalyptus leaves were used in poultices for wounds and inflammation.

• In China, diluted eucalyptus oil has been rubbed into painful inflamed joints in arthritis and gout, to relieve neuralgia, and rubbed into the temples for headaches.

A few drops of eucalyptus oil in hot water can be used to cleanse the air of infection in the sick room, or during a flu epidemic.

The eucalyptus is also known as the fever tree; its aromatic odour exerts an antiseptic effect in the area where it grows. It was planted in unhealthy marshes or swamps to dry up and purify these areas which were breeding grounds for disease.

Internal

The volatile oils in the leaves stimulate the circulation, enhancing blood flow to the skin and causing sweating. This clears toxins from the blood, lowers fever, and pushes out eruptions, so speeding the resolution of infections such as chicken pox and measles. A decoction of the leaves or an inhalation of a few drops of oil in a bowl of water can be used 2–3 times daily for colds, flu, and coughs; as an expectorant for asthma and chest infections including whooping cough, pneumonia, and bronchitis; and as a stimulating decongestant for catarrh and sinusitis. Eucalyptus's antiseptic properties are exerted throughout the respiratory tract as well as the digestive tract and, when taken in decoction, the leaves are an astringent remedy for bacillary dysentery, typhoid, diarrhoea, and vomiting. The volatile oils from the leaves are excreted through the urinary system, so a decoction will relieve infections such as cystitis and pyelonephritis. Recent research suggests that eucalyptus may lower blood sugar.

External

Eucalyptus oil can be used for a compress to apply to wounds, burns, ulcers, boils, and abscesses as an antiseptic, to stop bleeding, and to speed healing. Five drops mixed into a teaspoonful of almond or olive oil make a useful massage oil and chest rub for chest infections, bronchitis, and asthma. The dilute oil can be applied to the skin to ward off insects and treat infections such as ringworm and athlete's foot.

Few people can fail to be familiar with the fragrant smell of eucalyptus – the volatile oil that is exuded by the plant's bluish-green leaves. Both the leaves and oil have unique medicinal properties, but while the leaves may be taken internally in a decoction, the oil should only be used externally. An antiseptic and a febrifuge, eucalyptus was an old remedy for typhoid, scarlet fever, remittent fevers, malaria, and cholera. It was made into a wine, an aperitif to stimulate the appetite and aid digestion. A decoction of the leaves or a few drops of the oil mixed with water makes an effective gargle for sore throats.

EPSOM SALTS

A Mild and Safe Purgative Remedy

Properties

Purgative • Detoxifying

Folk remedies from the past
An Epsom salts bath once or twice a week will enhance the elimination of waste products via the skin. Dissolve 450g (1lb) of salts in a hot bath and give your body a friction rub all over with a bath brush. Finish with a cool shower, then dry with a rough towel until the skin glows. Recommended for gout and arthritis.

Epsom salts, or magnesium sulphate, are colourless, odourless, bitter-tasting crystals originally obtained from sea water. Unlike other purgatives, they do not cause nausea or griping, and when taken in a little water by mouth they are only slightly absorbed from the bowel. The rest remains in the bowel attracting water, which keeps the bowel distended and soon leads to a bowel movement. Their rapid action may cause defecation within half an hour. By drawing water from the body by osmosis, they are a useful means of excreting excess water. Epsom salts are used for chronic constipation, indigestion, biliousness, water retention causing high blood pressure, and clearing toxins and bacteria from the bowel.

GLYCERINE

Soothing to the Skin and Mucous Membranes

Properties

Antiseptic • Hygroscopic • Laxative • Expectorant • Demulcent

Folk remedies from the past
This sweet tasting, colourless, sticky liquid which was first isolated in 1779, is obtained by heating and distilling fats.

• Glycerine was once used to combat consumption and is an old household remedy to prevent and treat dry chapped skin, and also to soften hard skin.

Internally, one or two teaspoons of glycerine act as a laxative and relax the bowel, relieving colic and constipation. Glycerine is hygroscopic (draws water to it) and, once ingested, it distends the bowel and stimulates evacuation. It can also be taken to relieve indigestion and wind. Glycerine soothes mucous membranes and is a gentle expectorant in the respiratory system, particularly useful in dry, harsh, or tickly coughs. On the skin, it moisturises and soothes irritation and inflammation as in eczema, chilblains, and burns. A few drops of lavender oil mixed into dilute glycerine is an antiseptic hand lotion, healing cracks, sores, cuts, and whitlows. Equal parts glycerine and rosewater is good for chapped lips, rough skin, and sunburn.

MYRRH

A Most Precious Gift from Nature

Properties

Antiseptic • Astringent • Antibacterial • Antifungal • Analgesic • Expectorant
Decongestant • Anti-inflammatory

Myrrh is a shrubby tree, native to the Middle East. It has whitish-grey bark from which a yellow fluid flows, giving rise to a reddish-brown resin or gum. It is this which is dissolved in oils and tinctures. Myrrh was important to trade and commerce in the ancient world as it was very highly valued.

Internal

Myrrh is most often used as a tincture, which has a mixture of bitter, astringent, and pungent tastes. Its predominant effect is warming and stimulating, making it a great tonic if you are tired and run down. It increases circulation, dispels cold and weakness, and pushes out eruptions as it brings blood to the surface. It is also an expectorant and decongestant, and has been praised as a remedy for bronchitis, asthma, tuberculosis, colds, and catarrh. Its antiseptic and astringent properties give further benefit here. In the digestive tract it stimulates the appetite, improves digestion, relieves wind, and clears toxins and intestinal infections and parasites. Myrrh's warming qualities are of especial value in the reproductive system. It improves uterine circulation, restores delayed periods, and relaxes spasm. Use when childbirth is imminent to promote efficient contractions.

External

Here, the antiseptic and astringent properties of myrrh come into their own. A dilute tincture makes an excellent gargle for sore throats, tonsillitis, and laryngitis, and a mouthwash for inflamed gums and other oral infections. Use it as a douche for vaginal infections, such as thrush and trichomoniasis. Myrrh is also a wonderful tissue healer, speeding repair and soothing pain. It should be thought of for all minor injuries.

Folk remedies from the past

Myrrh was held in high esteem by the ancient Egyptians as one of the main ingredients for embalming the dead. Housewives used to burn pellets of myrrh to rid the house of fleas.

• The ancient Hebrews used myrrh as a purifying remedy to cleanse both body and spirit. As a medicine they relied on its antiseptic properties, while for spiritual purposes they burned it in incense. It was an ingredient of holy oils for anointing the tabernacle, altar, and sacred vessels.

• The ancient Greeks also revered myrrh. In one of their classic tales, a woman called Myrrha, the mother of the beautiful youth Adonis, was turned into a myrrh tree.

• In Ayurvedic medicine myrrh is believed to rejuvenate body and mind, reverse ageing, and prevent decay. It is used today to restore the female reproductive system and improve the blood.

CAUTION

Avoid in pregnancy; use only when birth is imminent.

WITCH HAZEL

A Wonderful Healing Astringent

Properties

Astringent • Anti-inflammatory

Folk remedies from the past

The North American Indians revered witch hazel for its astringent healing properties. Mixed with flax seed they used it for inflamed swellings and painful tumours. The branches made good divining rods for detecting underground water and metals – which may explain why it became known as "witch" hazel.

• In Britain and Europe, witch hazel was used as a general household remedy for scalds and burns, swellings and inflammation of the skin, and to stop bleeding. When dried, it was used as snuff to stop nose bleeds.

• Witch hazel used to be prescribed for uterine prolapse and a debilitated state after miscarriage or childbirth, to tone up the uterine muscles.

Witch hazel is an attractive deciduous shrub native to the eastern states of the US and Canada. It is often grown in gardens for its bright yellow flowers which appear in winter to enliven an otherwise bare garden. The bark, twigs, and leaves all seem to share the same medicinal properties.

Internal

The main action of witch hazel is astringent, due to the high levels of tannins it contains. This makes it an excellent remedy for bleeding, both internally and externally, and it has been used to stop bleeding from the lungs, stomach, uterus, and bowels. It can be taken for excessive menstruation and for uterine blood stagnation with a feeling of fullness, heaviness, and discomfort around a period. The tannins also check mucous discharges throughout the body, and have a toning, contracting action on the muscles and blood vessels, giving witch hazel a wonderfully wide variety of therapeutic uses. It is a good remedy for diarrhoea, dysentery, mucous colitis, and respiratory catarrh.

External

Apply either a decoction, tincture, or distillation of witch hazel to cuts and wounds, insect bites, and stings. The tannins not only stop bleeding, but also speed healing, reduce pain, inflammation, and swelling, and provide a protective coating on wounds to inhibit the development of infection. Use it as a mouthwash for bleeding gums, a gargle for sore throats and infections such as tonsillitis and laryngitis, an eyewash for sore eyes, and a douche for vaginal discharges. A poultice or compress will relieve burns, inflammatory skin problems, swollen engorged breasts, bed sores, bruises, sprains and strains, varicose veins and ulcers, and haemorrhoids.

As a lotion, witch hazel has many uses. Apply it to quell the pain, irritation, and swelling of insect and mosquito bites and stings, to relieve tender aching muscles, to lessen the pain of varicose veins and phlebitis, to soothe the itching of haemorrhoids, and to tighten the skin muscles and reduce broken skin capillaries. Mix it with rosewater to make a refreshing eye bath, or to soak eye pads for the relief of sore, tired, or inflamed eyes, including conjunctivitis. A lotion, decoction, or tincture can also be used as a douche for vaginal discharge.

GLOSSARY

Anaesthetic Deadens sensation and reduces pain
Analgesic Pain relieving
Anthelmintic Destroys or expels intestinal worms
Antibacterial Destroys or stops the growth of bacterial infections
Anticarcinogenic Retards/prevents the development of cancer
Antidepressant Relieves the symptoms of depression
Antifungal Treats fungal infections
Antihaemorrhagic Stops bleeding and haemorrhage
Antihistamine Neutralizes the effects of histamine in an allergic response
Anti-inflammatory Reduces inflammation
Antimicrobial Destroys or stops the growth of micro-organisms
Antioxidant Prevents damage by free radicals
Antirheumatic Relieves rheumatism/arthritis
Antiseptic Prevents putrefaction
Antiviral Destroys or stops the growth of viral infections
Aperient Laxative
Astringent Contracts tissue, drying, and reducing secretions or discharges
Bactericidal Able to destroy bacteria
Bitter Bitter-tasting substance which increases appetite, promotes digestion, and stimulates liver function
Cardiotonic A tonic for the heart
Carminative Eases cramping pains and expels flatulence
Cholagogue Increases flow of bile into the intestines
Decongestant Relieves congestion
Demulcent Soothes irritated tissues, especially mucous membranes
Depurative Cleanses and purifies the system, especially the blood
Detoxifying Eliminating toxins from the body
Diaphoretic Promotes sweating
Digestive Aids digestion
Diuretic Promotes the flow of urine
Emetic Causes vomiting
Endorphins Natural substances synthesized in the pineal gland which have an analgesic effect
Expectorant Promotes expulsion of mucus from respiratory tract
Febrifuge Reduces fever
Galactagogue Increases milk flow
Hygroscopic Tends to absorb water
Hypoglycaemic Reduces blood sugar
Hypotensive Reduces blood pressure
Laxative Promotes evacuation of the bowels
Oestrogenic Resembles the actions of oestrogen
Purgative Produces vigorous emptying of the bowels
Refrigerant Cooling substance
Relaxant Relaxes nerves/muscles
Restorative Restores normal physiological activity and energy
Rubefacient A gentle local irritation that produces redness of the skin and relieves inflammation
Sedative Reduces nervousness and anxiety, induces sleep
Stimulant Produces energy and increases circulation
Tonic Invigorates and tones the body and promotes well-being
Vasodilator Widens blood vessels, lowering blood pressure and bringing blood to the skin surface

RECOMMENDED READING

Diet and Nutrition Rudolph Ballantine MD, Himalayan Institute, Pennsylvania, USA 1978
Nutritional Medicine Dr. Stephen Davies & Dr. Alan Steward. Pan Books 1987
Mind, Body and Immunity Rachel Charles. Methuen, 1990
An ABC of Natural Beauty Dian Dincin Buchman. Duckworth 1976
Herbal Cosmetics Liz Sanderson. Fontana/Collins 1979
Natural Remedies for Common Ailments Constance Mellor. Granada 1975
Food Pharmacy Jean Carper. Simon & Schuster Ltd. 1989
New Dimensions in Health David A. Phillips. Angus & Robertson, 1983
Superfoods Michael van Stratten & Barbara Griggs. Dorling Kindersley 1990
Introduction to Pharmacology J. J. Lewis. Livingston & Co. 1964
Folk Medicine D. C. Jarvis, W. H. Allen, London 1960
Herbs for Common Ailments Anne McIntyre, Gaia Books 1988
The Complete New Herbal Richard Mabey, Elm Tree Books 1988
Folk Medicine Jaques Veissid. Quartet Books 1979
Grandmother's Cures Dennis Prince. Fontana 1991
Grandmother's Secrets Jean Palaiseul. Penguin 1976
Drugs, Medicines and Man H.Brown, Unwin University Books 1963
Super Immunity for Kids Leo Gallard MD, Bloomsbury, 1989
Modern Herbal Mrs.M.Grieve. Penguin, 1984
Herbs and Things Jeanne Rose. Grosset and Dunlop. Workman Pub.Co. New York 1972
Guide to Medicinal Plants Schauenberg & Paris, Lutterworth Press 1977
Health Secrets of Plants and Herbs Maurice Messegne. Collins, 1979
A Country Herbal Lesley Gordon. Peerage Books 1984
Nature's Medicines Richard Lucas. Parker Pub.Co., New York 1966
Natural Beauty Lorna Horrocks. Angus & Robertson 1980
Encyclopaedia of Common Natural Ingredients used in Food, Drugs and Cosmetics Albert Y. Leung, John Wiley & Sons, New York 1980
The Energetics of Western Herbs Vol 1 & 2 Peter Holmes. Artemis Press USA 1989
The Yoga of Herbs Dr. Vasant Lad & David Frantey. Lotus Press. 1986
Elixirs of Life Mrs. Leyel. Stuart & Watkins Ltd., 1970
The Herb Society's Complete Medicinal Herbal Penelope Ody MNIMH. Dorling Kindersley, 1993
Healing Foods Miriam Polunin. Dorling Kindersley, 1997
The plants we need to eat Jeanette Ewin. Thorsons, 1997
Foods that Harm, Foods that Heal Reader's Digest, 1996

INDEX

Also published by Gaia Books in the same series

Aromatherapy for Common Ailments

Shirley Price

ISBN 1 85675 005 1

Beautiful photography and clear, informative text from best-selling author Shirley Price provide an invaluable reference on treating a wide range of ailments, with advice on using home treatments.

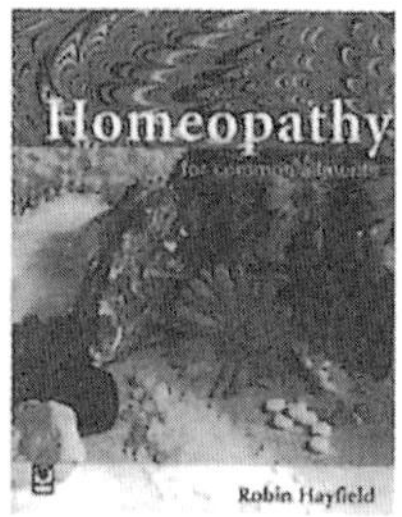

Homeopathy for Common Ailments

Robin Hayfield

ISBN 1 85675 021 3

Homeopathic remedies are safe, natural forms of treatment. This book helps you select remedies for physical and emotional problems, from coughs and croup to anxiety, chicken pox to hayfever. Ideal for children's treatments.

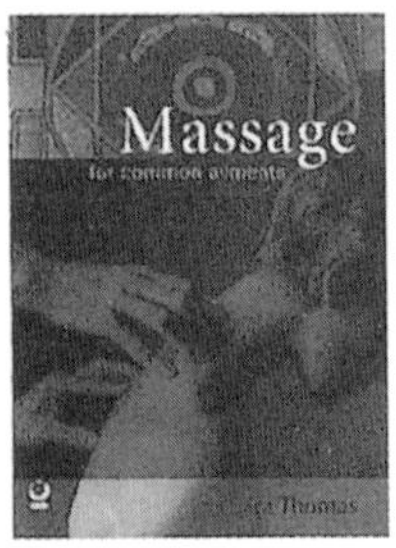

Massage for Common Ailments

Sara Thomas

ISBN 1 85675 031 0

Simple massage techniques for effective and precise treatment of everyday problems, both physical and mental.

Herbs for Common Ailments

Anne McIntyre

ISBN 1 85675 055 8

Herbs for Common Ailments responds to today's renewed search for simple, effective and natural treatments. It shows how to choose and use herbs for everyday illnesses.

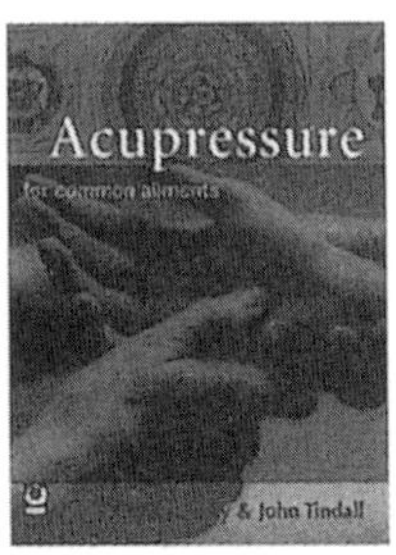

Acupressure for Common Ailments

Chris Jarmey & John Tindall

ISBN 1 85675 015 9

By applying pressure to specific points on the body you can stimulate subtle energy to boost the immune system and alleviate many common ailments.

To request a full catalogue of titles published by Gaia Books please call 01453 752985, fax 01453 752987 or write to Gaia Books, 20 High Street, Stroud, Gloucestershire, GL5 1AS
e-mail address: gaiabook@star.co.uk
Internet address: http://www.gaiabooks.co.uk